D0595194

Tony,
Thank you for
years of service
and fun~
Susan Larboin

OUT OF MY WORLD, INTO THEIRS

Susan Langlois

Book Design by Conch Custom
Published with assistance from Conch Custom,
an imprint of Nauset Press.
Publishing contact: info@nausetpress.com

ISBN-13: 978-1545235317
ISBN-10: 1545235317

For Mom and Dad, who told me early on to reach for the stars.
For Ray, Randy and Conner, my motivation to reconnect.

★ ★ ★

And for everyone
Who has ever been
on the outside,
looking in.

The wound is the place where the Light enters you. —Rumi

TABLE OF CONTENTS

BIG BEND LANDSCAPE (LEFT), Susan Langlois

PREFACE

*I*n 2011 I walked away from my world. Without thinking twice, I left behind a black and white life of confusion and stepped into the warm, glowing world of sound.

Here I am. Hear I am.

I wrote this book to reach others who are struggling in the world I had left behind. However, adversity is something that everyone understands, and my struggles are representative of the challenges that we all face in overcoming our limitations in the world.

Some of the descriptions were painful to recall, but each chapter released mountains of trapped emotion—words of hope, despair, defeat, spirit, strength, perseverance, and ultimately triumph. No longer alone, I am connected to my family, my world, my life. No longer lost, I am here now—because I can hear now.

1. ACTIVATION DAY

Time is like the silky sand,
a canvas of natural beauties.
One by one, the grains add up
Landscaping life with memories.

— S.L.

MAY 24, 2011

Static knocking me out of my chair like an exploding amplifier. Beeps, shocking every nerve in my body like live wires. Whistles, screeching through my brain like nails on a chalkboard.

Silence, like the mysterious prelude to a movie.

And then, something else. Sound?

Through the screeching, scratching, and whistling, there was a faint, "Can you hear me now?"

The terrifying moment skidded to a stop. I had heard something! This was Activation Day.

I was sitting in my audiologist's office, exactly two weeks after the implant. The wait for Activation Day had been slow and frustrating because the surgery resulted in the total deafness of the implanted ear. Before the implant, I had been able to hear booms and bangs with my hearing aid, and going from that to absolutely silence was difficult. I prayed that it would all change when my bionic ear was activated.

I had my doubts. Forty years of begging, pleading, and bargaining for a miracle had never produced any relief. But the cochlear implant changed everything, producing whistles, beeps, static ... and then sound. After several tense adjustments, the moment of truth had finally arrived.

"Can you hear me, Susan?"

It was the voice of Sherri, my audiologist. I was hearing her voice in its entirety—all the sounds of each word, not just the crackled, faint bits and pieces I was used to. Although her words were filled with startling new whistling sounds I didn't recognize, I understood the message. She was asking me a question and it deserved an answer!

This moment was an instant connection of words between two people, almost as powerful as the human touch. It's what I had been praying, begging, and bargaining for all my life. I wish I could have had a clever answer, but all I could say was, "Oh my gosh, oh my gosh, oh my gosh!"

Sherri had found just the right mapping for my new bionic ear, one that sent joy directly to my heart. She just smiled, talked to me, watched my expressions, and waited for it to sink in. My husband and son, sitting nearby for support, looked on uneasily. As my tears turned to sobs and then smiles, they alternated between confusion and concern. But they had nothing to worry about.

These were tears of happiness.

Finally catching my breath, I said, "Yes, I can hear."

"I can hear."

"I can hear!"

After Sherri left the room to give us some private time, my husband, son, and I stared at each other. We didn't know what to say to one another. Then, after a few seconds of staring, we all laughed.

"Is it working?" my husband finally asked.

His voice was very different, rich with depth but still filled with bells, whistles, and beeps. It had more clarity, though, and was much easier to follow than Sherri's, because I was so familiar with his speaking style, articulation, inflection, and tone. For many years, my husband had been patient enough to speak as loud as I had needed while my hearing deteriorated. Although I had lost the ability to hear much of his voice in recent years, there was still enough there to recognize him when my bionic ear was turned on.

"You sound like a robot, but I hear you," I told him as we smiled at each other. The smile that had taken over my face in the audiologist's office stayed put long after the activation. Every single experience from that moment on offered something new.

Along with the actual sound of voices, it was important that I become specifically accustomed, almost programmed, to all of these fresh, new sounds—including those that had almost knocked me out of my chair. The abrasive static, intermittent beeps, and piercing whistles, as I came to discover, were not simply strange, irritating noises. They were authentic sounds that I had simply never heard before. If sounds were like keys on a piano, I was now accessing 100% of them after a lifetime of being only able to hear the last quarter, at best, and most of these new sounds were unrecognizable.

Sherri came back into her office and double-checked my bionic equipment, which included a remote control. She confirmed my comfort levels one last time before packing me up to go home. Activation Day was complete. It was time to walk outside and start the adventure of learning how to hear.

I was incapable of understanding the vastness of this process, that learning how to hear would require a lifetime of study and practice, and I would only be as successful as I was determined. Learning to hear would not be easy, but it would be one of the most rewarding adventures of my life.

At forty-six years old, I was no longer trapped in my own world, but a part of the wider world of sound. Leaving the silence marked the end of a very long, distressing chapter in my life with an explosion of joy and wonder. That day is appreciated, but so are all the days that came before it. Because God had placed me in tough situations all through my life, I was prepared for the lengthy, complex task of mastering sound and speech. Had I not endured those forty-six years, I may never have found my way to a cochlear implant.

Accepting defeat at any point could have closed many doors, limited my opportunities, and weakened my faith. Forty-six years of adversity strengthened my spirit, taught me perseverance, and prepared me for the day I would wake up almost completely deaf— and also for the day I would nearly be knocked off my chair by sound.

I perched my elbows atop the cochlear implant suitcase as my face rested in my cupped hands. Slipping into a daydream, I revisited the emotional moments when sounds were taken from me.

II. MAGIC BEANS

It's official, she's in grade school now.

Papers have been signed—

trying hard to read and write,

this rookie child will shine!

— S.L.

1970

WHACK

WHACK

WHACK

*T*he paddle smacked me three times.

Each swat stung like a thousand bee stings, and the sound of the paddle slapped shamefully in my ears. I was paddled in secret several times that year. Each time, my first-grade teacher would pull me into the closet to administer her punishment. At least it was over quickly. I don't remember crying or being scared. I was just ashamed, sad, and confused, although I wasn't able to articulate any of these things. Confusion was my normal state, having never been able to fully understand the world around me. So I stopped trying to make sense of the nonsense.

Instead of connecting with the outside world, I formed a connection within myself, singing pretend songs with my limited speech and making up rhymes in my head. This coping mechanism kept me going for decades. I was my best friend, and my only friend. It was much easier than trying to hear all the voices of those around me. Speech rarely made sense, and everyday events rarely had meaning. So I never saw those first three swats coming.

Forty years later, I still don't know why she paddled me. The subsequent paddlings were just as inexplicable as the first one. Three spankings in first grade with no proof and no one to validate it made the whole experience seem more fiction than fact. But the stings from the board were too real to deny, and the memory haunted me for years. Certainly it would have been easier to simply forget!

Why did I cling to the memory? The spankings were painful, not fatal. The stinging humiliation in first grade triggered the development of a rich host of hard-earned character traits. The outcome was faith. This is the real story! Life's beatings do hurt, but despair is the birth of faith and hope. My faith was born during that first paddling. It was the most surprising of the three because it happened suddenly—no warning, no cause, and no motive that I could see. A few years later a classmate briefly spoke to me about the incident, explaining that the whacks had stemmed from some "magic beans."

Initially, those beans were called "motivator beans." Miss Teacher, as I referred to her, used the beans to encourage good behavior, rewarding students with a bean for completed work, walking quietly in line, or sitting quietly in class. On that day, she saw me stealing beans from her desk. She asked me about the theft and it was my misfortune that all my answers were wrong, pushing her to the point of losing control. What exactly did I say that angered her? Fifteen years later, I finally got the answer.

In 1987 I was teaching my own class, drawing connections between students and teachers, and reflecting on the insights of each. I linked those professional reflections to the countless conversations I'd had with my mother, conversations that centered around the effects of my hearing impairment on my social behavior. In doing this, we cleared up years and years of misunderstandings and miscommunications. Relatives and friends told me that on a great many occasions as a child, I did not respond to directions and often walked away from adults who were talking to me. Armed with this pinch of knowledge, I understood how I ended up in that closet, bent over with my teacher whacking my backside. *I will never agree that it had to happen, but I understand how it happened.*

Those three paddlings had little to do with the magic beans. They were not the result of my answers to Miss Teacher's questions. The whacks had everything to do with what I didn't say. I kept my beans in a baby food jar on top of my desk, as we all did. One day, some of my beans fell on the floor and were lost. The next day several beans appeared on Miss Teacher's desk. I was convinced they were my lost beans, though it's possible that they weren't.

I didn't ask for them back because they were already mine. As a hard of hearing six-year-old child, I rarely spoke to anyone. My shyness was almost debilitating, and I never wanted to be noticed. So I waited for my teacher to leave the room, then plucked them off her desk. Carefully placing them back in my jar, I felt that this was their rightful home and I was happy.

This must have taken place in the clear view of my teacher—she knew right away what I had done. She walked over from the door and stood over me as I was busy doing handwriting pages in my workbook. I was always proud of my handwriting and continued dotting my i's and crossing my t's as she stood over me. Was I supposed to acknowledge her? I was too shy to make eye contact and hoped she would walk away if I made all my best letters for her. She didn't. Kneeling down to my eye level, she announced something to the class, looking me straight in the eye.

"Class, some beans have disappeared off my desk—they must be magic beans."

It made no sense to me so I ignored it, as I always did when my world didn't make sense. Looking down at my workbook, I felt relief in the lovely lines of the alphabet. This must have been frustrating to Miss Teacher.

As I continued writing, she walked back to the classroom door, watching me closely. Miss Teacher did not take her eyes off me as I completed the workbook page, written as neatly as I could. Instinctively, I knew she was either talking to me or about me. Emotionally, I was unable to attend to either. I was focused on my handwriting because that is all I had. Perhaps Miss Teacher had been calling my name several times. Perhaps she had been giving me directions. I never heard it.

I did notice the other kids looking over at me though. Before I realized what was happening, Miss Teacher escorted me, holding my arm, into the hallway. It looked as if she was talking to me, but everything she said sounded like the adults in a Charlie Brown cartoon, "*wah wah wah.*"

My limited ability to hear speech had resulted in a limited ability to speak. Because I couldn't hear well, I could not speak well. So I said nothing. Instead of a student/teacher conference that Miss Teacher might have been seeking, I zoned out of the world and into my mind, where comfort lived. She continued to stare at me as I looked at her blankly, safely away from her world. I didn't know what else to do but hang my head. Suddenly I was tired. So tired.

Zoning out was my way of disconnecting from stressful situations. It's a coping mechanism for many people who don't understand or know how deal with what is happening around them. Making eye contact with an angry adult was a horrifying idea, so I waited with my head bowed, waiting for whatever this was to end. Miss Teacher never received the response she had been looking for, or the respect of being listened to. She did the only thing she could think of—she took the paddle and started whacking.

And I did the only thing I could think of. I sang a song to myself, and took my first step into faith. I kept singing until Miss Teacher stopped spanking.

> *Jesus loves the little children,*
> *All the children of the world,*
> *Red and yellow, black and white,*
> *They are precious in his sight,*
> *Jesus loves the little children of the world.*

I sang the entire song through once. And then, just like that, there were no more whacks.

Among the many common misunderstandings about hearing-impaired individuals is how our lack of reaction to others is a reflection of our lack of respect. Miss Teacher's misunderstanding of children with this type of disability caused her to behave badly. And she had no reason to think that I couldn't hear because I had passed my hearing test! Incredibly, I would pass the school hearing "test" every single year from the first grade on.

Regardless of the fact that she didn't know about my hearing problem, I don't know that Miss Teacher ever tried to identify a reason for my disconnection. Had she dug a little deeper than the surface, she might have come a little closer to understanding—and I might have been spared those spankings.

Another misconception about the hearing-impaired population is that we have "selective hearing." It's easy for some to believe that hard-of-hearing kids are really sneaky, fibbing little rascals. The truth is that most hearing-impaired children don't know they can't hear; they won't ask you what you said if they didn't hear it in the first place. I don't remember saying, even once, "I didn't hear you" or "what did you say?" As a matter of fact, I don't remember much about those early days at school except those whacks and how they opened up my faith.

Fortunately, I did learn something from those paddlings. Every dark cloud has a silver lining and my silver lining was personal growth, even at the age of six years old. I learned that I unquestionably had to figure out how to read people in order to have an appropriate response to them. Or at least have some response. This meant that I needed to learn how to talk. It was a frightening idea for a girl who couldn't even think of a response to "hello." But going into second grade, it was a clear necessity that I voice a response when spoken to.

So I paid closer attention to teachers, trying hard to be a good girl. I said, "please, thank you, yes ma'am, and no ma'am". I listened hard during lessons, and though I regularly became lost in the muffled sounds and broken words, I tried extra hard to look like I was following along. I learned to nod politely when I knew I should, and feign comprehension when I could. I never raised my hand to offer an answer, preparing instead a generic response in case I was called upon. I learned the pattern of round robin reading, preparing for my turn on the correct page or paragraph. Instinctively I began learning how to read lips, gestures, and facial expressions.

That was my world in 1970. I was the middle child of three in a Southern family of five. We had membership in a Baptist church, and fellowship with various family friends. I was always on the outside looking in. I looked like any other kid, but I felt much different as I revolved through the daily cycles of being confused, observant, and lost. This unsettling environment was not mine for admission so I left it, opting instead to connect with a world more accepting of me—and only me, because I was the only one in it. I had withdrawn. I found temporary relief from muddled language and increasing isolation. I found a safety blanket in my own solitude because I could hear my own voice there. I talked to myself in the safety of my consciousness. Here, in the absence of unfinished speech and muffled sounds, I was comfortable.

★ ★ ★

I became a chameleon in the classroom for years, not wanting to be noticed or looked at. I tried a few new activities with a bit of success. All the girls were joining a drill team in fifth grade, so I became a dancer too, with my mother's encouragement. Never mind that you have to be able to hear the music! My mother said I could do anything I wanted to do—and I believed her and became a Cowgirl Dancer Girl.

Cowgirls had one purpose: to dance for the Cowboys, a youth football team. During dance practice, which was held near the football field, I felt my way through the music by tuning in to the beat on the ground. For the first time, I noticed that I could even feel the music in my fingertips. I felt I had crept successfully into "their" world and I was happy being there.

I danced confidently, moving in sync to the vibration of the ground, believing in myself as a dancing Cowgirl. Then everything skidded to a stop when a fellow Cowgirl with big hair on top of her head and blue glitter on her eyelids walked right up to me. She stood six inches from my face and asked if I was retarded. I wished that I couldn't hear her or see her. But I could. I wished that I could disappear from the practice field. But I couldn't. I wished that I was bold enough to answer her. But I wasn't.

Too shy to answer such a terrible question, I ran off and sat in the grass looking up to the sky. My private world, isolated as it may have been, was like a ship sailing away on peaceful ocean of faith. Everything would be okay there, where the earth cushioned my heartache and the sky swallowed my despair. So I lay down into the carpet of soft grass, sucked on a three-leaf clover I had plucked from the earth and watched the clouds float peacefully across the afternoon sky. I went home after practice as if nothing had ever happened. I obediently continued dancing with the Cowgirls, carefully avoiding the girl with the big hair and blue glitter, until the season finally ended. That was my first and last year of dancing.

My sisters and I also tried softball in a youth league for preteens. I had never been thought of as an athlete, and for good reason. Without hearing aids or glasses, I was essentially blind and deaf, and I made very few good plays in practice and none at all during our games. Softballs were attracted to me, though. They shot through the air in my direction many times, once even smacking me right on the cheek. I finished the season with a little bit of pride in the fact that I hadn't quit. But just as it was with dancing, that was my first and last year of softball. I was ready to leave sports behind and go back to school, where I was safe from big-haired girls and flying balls.

When fifth grade began, I quickly became the teacher's pet. Eleven years old and ready to be acknowledged, I was pleased to be noticed by my teacher. She had won me over by giving shiny smiley stickers if I picked up trash, touching my shoulder as she walked by my desk, and by smiling, smiling, smiling. She smiled at me every time I looked up at her.

But after the first week of school, she took it to a new level. She was asking me to do things, and that made me nervous. I had never been asked to deliver envelopes, pass out papers, or do other secretarial jobs. Kids loved to do these things, so on one hand I was very pleased. But I was also unsure of myself—and agitated because I didn't completely understand all of this.

★　★　★

I knew my limitations, even at eleven years old. I had made plenty of mistakes at home when told to do something that I hadn't heard correctly. If that happened at school, it would be much worse. Everyone would discover how dumb I was, should I mess up.

And mess up I did. On several occasions, I delivered things to the wrong person. "Weren't you listening, sweetheart?" my teacher would ask me. Timid as a mouse, I would smile shyly and respond with a quiet "I'm sorry." I was constantly worried that my secret would be exposed. I didn't know half of what was going on, and I didn't know why I didn't know!

After each correction, I learned to pay twice as much attention when teachers repeated their instructions, how to study faces more intensely for lip reading, and the art of problem solving through the process of elimination. It worked much of the time. But even then, after listening as hard as I could and earnestly reading lips, I still delivered things to the wrong destination a second time. When this happened, my plan was this: walk around politely showing what I was supposed to deliver to any adult passing by. Each time, a patient teacher stopped to help and saved my day.

I remained the teacher's pet all year long—until the very last week of school, when my teacher ran out of patience with me. Despite my incredible shyness, I had been chosen to narrate the fifth-grade recital. Everything had been going smoothly. I memorized my lines, paid attention during rehearsals, was always ready to recite my lines on cue, and performed very well during our practices in front of the whole fifth grade. I felt such pride, as if I had been walking across a tightrope over the Grand Canyon and I was making it across! I had almost made it safely to the other side!

Almost. Just before the last rehearsal, students were buzzing with excitement. My teacher came to me with her clipboard in hand. By the stride of her walk in my direction and the notes she made quickly on her clipboard, I decided she would be asking for my help. After all, I was the teacher's pet and starting to feel proud of it. Anticipating as I always did, I predicted that she had forgotten something in our classroom and was about to ask me to go and get it, whatever it was.

Amid the buzzing of the students, the pianist rehearsing her part, and adults chatting, my teacher's voice never made it to my ears. Her voice disappeared as it exited her mouth, like a firefly disappears in the dark. As she spoke to me, I stared at her in confusion. In my world, nothing made sense—so this actually made perfect sense. Abnormal was normal. The only thing I did hear her say was "okay?" at the end. I nodded and said, "okay" back. I was going to fix this, and that's why it was going to be "okay."

I walked to my classroom and opened the door. I was nervous but keenly observant as I looked around for clues to this dilemma. I quietly tiptoed over to my teacher's desk, searching for something, anything that looked as if it might belong at rehearsal. I found no props, no scripts—nothing out of the ordinary. I decided to put my "last resort" plan into action—walking the halls and hoping that someone would stop and offer to help. But on that particular day, there were no adults in the halls.

I paced hallway after hallway, each one with more worry than the last, until I finally ended up back at the rehearsal in the cafeteria, where I knew they were waiting—on me. My stomach churned as I tiptoed in, trying not be noticed. But my teacher, along with all the other fifth-grade teachers and aides, had been looking for me.

My teacher called out something to me from across the large room. I had no response because I had no idea what she'd said. I was too scared even to move.

She took the microphone. "Where have you been?!" she screamed. That, I did hear.

The entire group of fifth-graders turned and looked in my direction. My teacher, the only teacher who had ever chosen me to be her favorite, angrily marched over to me, snatched off my "Narrator" pin, and scolded me for what seemed like hours. I blinked hard, swallowed the lump in my throat, and waited for it to end. The only special relationship with a teacher I had ever enjoyed was now ruined because she had discovered how stupid I really was. Finally she pointed vigorously to the group of my classmates standing on the steps in front of the stage, where I was sent for the remainder of our rehearsal. I was no longer the narrator. I was no longer the teacher's pet.

And thank God I would no longer be in the fifth grade in a week's time. Summer would save me. When school let out a few days later, I ran as far away as I could from that elementary school, faithful that there would be life after humiliation. Because there was no other choice, I trusted in hope and looked optimistically to the next adventure: intermediate school. I just knew that something was good coming up.

A few weeks later, I discovered recorded music. I had always liked songs—what I could hear of them—filling in the empty patches with my own made-up assortment of words and sounds. I sang all the time whether I was in bed or in the shower. Because I couldn't actually hear much of my own voice, I didn't realize that anyone else could hear me either, probably to the entertainment of those around. But professional music made a dramatic debut one day as I lay in my driveway.

I had been looking up at the sky watching the clouds float slowly past a full moon, which I was drawn to. I had been daydreaming about many things: junior high, boys, and whether the moon really had a man in it, as I had dreamed of several times. If the moon did have a man in it, I was convinced that he was my friend. Closing my eyes, I daydreamed of a white wedding with Mr. Moon, on the moon.

Suddenly there was an interruption—it was my dad, who had walked out of the house and over to where I lay in the driveway. "Hey," he said in a loud voice, startling me out of my fantasy. He smiled as he handed something over to me. I later learned that he had received it as a "fan appreciation gift" at a major league baseball game the day before. I had no idea what it was, but politely thanked him.

The "fan appreciation gift" was a white plastic box-shaped contraption. Dad said something to me in response to my thank you, but of course I did not respond as I tried to process the little pieces I had heard of what he said. I continued to look at the thing, unknowingly holding it upside down. He must have realized my inexperience with this type of device, so he took it from my hands, turned it right side up, and flipped a switch. He moved a dial back and forth until he was satisfied, then gave it back to me. I still didn't know what it was or what to do with it.

"Can't you hear it? It's a radio," he said, slowly moving the contraption up to my ear. When the radio was an inch away, he removed his hand and watched my reaction. My eyes almost popped out of my head! Music!

Dad smiled at me broadly, entertained and delighted at my excitement over the AM radio. While he made his way back to the house, I pressed the radio into my ear as hard as I could. How I wished it were louder! I started examining the white box more thoroughly for a way to turn the volume up. Finding two dials on the side of the box, I slowly turned one of them, but lost the music. Gently I moved the first dial back into place, then reached for the second one. Delicately, I turned the dial from five to nine. The music jumped out at me! The song slapped me in the face, but I liked it! Pressing the radio to my ear, I sat listening to the songs in the driveway, not moving, barely breathing, and watching the clouds move across the sky.

At twelve years old, I was hearing real music: complete with drums, trumpets, bass guitars, and pianos for the first time—and it was magical. I listened for hours. At the time, I didn't foresee the harmful physical effects of listening to music with the volume on the highest setting. Sometimes I pressed the radio as far as I could get it into my ear. Later on in my teen years, I was told that loud music would damage my ears, but the long-term effects didn't matter because of the profound impact that music was making on my life.

Music made me feel alive, releasing the joy, excitement, and love that had been buried underneath my confusion. Songs had a way of reaching me when people couldn't. It felt so good to be reached! As a teen, I went to the music store in the mall to look at the sheet music and learn the lyrics so I could sing along to my favorite songs. I listened to music as much as I could, turning up the volume as loud as I needed to experience it.

In sixth grade, I took another leap and joined the choir. A dynamic choir director led all of the intermediate choirs. She had a knack for getting the best performance out of her students. The secret to her success was this: she was one scary choir teacher! I liked her as much as I was scared of her. She had some frightening ways, but I knew she liked me because I was the recipient of many of her favorable nods and smiles. I was a good little girl—quiet, obedient, attentive, at least in appearance.

She didn't have a pointed nose or a pointy black hat. But she was very skilled, demanding, and had high expectations. Perhaps these character traits made her scary to kids who were learning to set goals, aim high, and expect more. In fact, my music teacher greatly elevated my singing skills and music reading. The one particular trait that affected me the most was her intensely powerful voice.

She demonstrated the music with ear-splitting volume, enabling me to hear my part before ever attempting it myself. I had a gift of being able to match each note very well once I could hear it for a split second. My mind could memorize it after that. Her thundering vocal chords also helped me as she taught us how read music and decode music symbols. Had she not spoken loud enough, I would never have figured out all the letters, lines, dots, and stems. From the reaction of my classmates, I suspect she was not the most popular teacher in junior high. But she helped me learn music for the solo and ensemble contest. In return for teaching me with such strength, I practiced my songs day and night, in my head and out loud. Though I couldn't actually hear all of it, I could hear enough to get by. Through behavior modification, Mrs. Maddox trained my voice to hit the right note. When I was off, her eyes bulged and it didn't feel good. When I was right on target, she smiled proudly. We made a good team and I did well enough at the contest to earn singing medals in both sixth and seventh grades. Music had reached into my world regularly and beckoned me out. I opened my ears and my mouth because of my choir teacher, singing my way through junior high.

I believe that music has the ability to transcend the physical when it goes beyond the ear and reaches into your heart. One Sunday in sixth grade, music did that at church. My mom let me sit with her instead of going to Sunday School. After the greetings and introduction of visitors, which of course I did not hear, a lady with big brown hair walked to the pulpit. But I could clearly see her face from our pew, which was front and center, luckily for me. I studied her features, wondering what was next in the "program," as I called it.

The large majestic wooden organ began playing, and though I could not make out the melody, I enjoyed the vibration and loud gonging noise it made. Then, very gracefully, the lady with the big hair opened her mouth and began to sing. It was loud, loving, passionate and beautiful.

This was a voice so loud and so clear, I was capturing the words! I believe it was a miracle that was meant to reach me. Even though I couldn't hear, on this day I did hear. Her words reached me, touch me, spoke to me, and changed me. They soared through the air, touching hearts and caressing souls. As the song went on, I realized Who it was and what He was telling me: I am loved, I am safe, and I will never walk alone. And on she sang, verse after verse as I found fellowship with the Lord ...

Amazing grace, how sweet the sound,
that saved a wretch like me.
I once was lost, but now am found,
was blind but now I see.

Instantly, it became part of me. Once I learned to sing it, the music never stopped. Even later on in my life when I heard very little, if anything, I still caroled "Amazing Grace"!

A few months after that Sunday a song from my little white box stirred my heart again, almost as powerfully as "Amazing Grace"

had. I sang the few lines I knew until I was able to run to the music store and learn them all. I sang the song all the time—outside, inside, standing in the street, riding my bike, in the shower, and in my dreams. This song was more than a story set to a piano medley; it was an important message. My heart was jubilant with love, and I deeply wanted to share it. When I sang this new song, love was everywhere, love was in everything, and love was for everyone.
I told my mother that I wished to sing it to Jesus. She made it happen, orchestrating my first, and only, church solo. Even though I wasn't even in the choir, my mother worked her magic and I was set to sing my song the next Sunday. Incredibly, I wasn't nervous until just moments before I was to begin.

Stepping up to the pulpit, I was surprised to see all the people in the pews, sitting there silently—looking at me. It was an odd view from the other side of the podium looking out. Adding to the peculiarity of the moment was the organ, which sounded very unusual from where I was standing. It didn't actually sound like an organ at all. But with or without the distractions, I was going to sing from my heart. So, at twelve years old, I put myself out there for all to see and sang Debbie Boone's "You Light Up My Life"—my personal thank you to Jesus.

When it was over, I felt peaceful, happy, and relieved. I felt strong, and nothing else mattered. The experience was amazing, like it was the best day of my life. The explosion of my musical life in junior high was followed by a surge in social skills. Certain aspects of community were making sense. As I opened up to budding relationships, a small group of girls became close friends. I was still shy, but I was able to be kind to others and laugh with them. We must have spent the night at each other's house almost every weekend that summer, staying up late or all night.

Worn out from the enormous effort required of reading situations through gestures, picking out individual voices in a gathering of girls, and filling in the gaps of things I didn't understand, my nights usually ended by midnight, to the delight of the other girls. Our sleepovers always included practical jokes—sometimes I joyfully took part in them, laughing till my sides ached. Many times, I knew what was waiting for me as my eyelids became heavy. Falling asleep early at a teenage sleepover usually meant my girls were going to be ready with a practical joke. It was like a bonus! And I must say, waking up with my hand in water and my undergarments flying around on the ceiling fan made for some unforgettable teenage memories. It was innocent and comical, and I was so happy!

What I couldn't hear, I didn't worry about because there were so many of us that nobody noticed. I don't recall anyone ever asking what was wrong with me, why I wasn't responding, or if I was retarded. As a shy chameleon, I was quietly blending in with this group of good-natured, loving girls. I wished that summer would never end.

But it did. When the summer of 1979 ended, I was ready for high school.

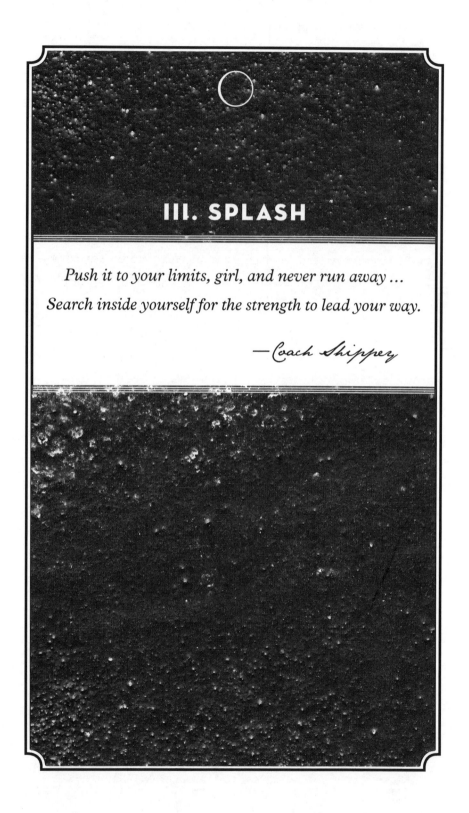

III. SPLASH

Push it to your limits, girl, and never run away ...
Search inside yourself for the strength to lead your way.

—Coach Shippey

1979

*H*aving made the team, I spent most of my freshman year learning how to swim—and how to make friends with a large group of kids. I wanted to learn how to do it and I knew I would to do more than just watch. I would have to talk. Still painfully shy, I rarely spoke to new people outside my small circle of friends. I had to do better.

The very first new person who received a response was my swim coach. He had no idea that I couldn't hear his low mumbling voice. He had reached out to me several times but I had never answered. Even still, he continued to speak to me, and I began figuring out his speech patterns and predicting his dialogue. Then one day I was late to second-period swimming class after a dentist appointment. The JV team was already in the pool swimming laps as I gave him my "Admit to Class" slip. Coach mumbled, as was his usual style, something about where I'd been. I replied that I had been to the dentist. I even looked him in the eyes! This small exchange was a huge accomplishment for me that I will never forget because it was the beginning of a connection between coach and student that lasted a lifetime.

As a ninth-grade JV swimmer, a particular set of challenges emerged. I was unable to distinguish voices as they blended in with the splashes of pool water, bouncing off the walls of the natatorium.

Thinking that this uncomfortable situation would go away as I figured everything out over time, I shrugged it off and followed the lead of the other swimmers. But I was unable to function successfully and independently during swim practice because I could not hear my coach, my teammates, the workout buzzer, or even the school bell. In the water and alone in my world, I faced a truth I could no longer run from. Something was wrong with me. That's all I knew.

I didn't know what was wrong. I didn't know how to fix it.I didn't know what to do.

So I kept swimming, moving forward, going somewhere, anywhere—since there was no other place to go. I swam my way right into my sophomore year.

★　　★　　★

I am unsure of how it materialized, but one day in tenth grade I ended up in the office of one of the most noted ear, nose, and throat specialists in Texas. Conceivably a teacher or nurse contacted my parents with concerns after I failed a hearing test. I just don't know. But at age fifteen, someone had a hunch that I wasn't being scatterbrained and aloof—something else was going on.

In the ENT's office, my parents answered a few questions. As always, I listened—sort of, and looked fully attentive. The doctor made inquiries into my medical background and my parents responded to his questions while I sat there in silence. Then the doctor ushered me into a padded room resembling a mental institution. It was awkward and uncomfortable, like I was going to be put into a straight jacket. This, as I discovered, was a soundproof room where a second doctor—an audiologist—would perform a professional hearing test. He tested me right there in the office and voila, we had answers. I was diagnosed as hearing impaired.

The audiologist described my hearing impairment as "ski slope" hearing loss, which meant that I had mild hearing loss in the low frequencies but considerable loss in the higher frequencies, with some frequencies in the normal range completely inaudible to me.

Specifically, I was deaf to certain high-pitched sounds, and others, such as the letters /f/, /c/, /b/, /d/, and /z/ were extremely hard to distinguish. This made it difficult, sometimes impossible to understand speech. In effect, I could hear, but not well enough to understand speech unless it was amplified. The audiologist told my parents that I could expect my hearing loss to deteriorate, but he could not predict the rate of deterioration. It was funny to hear him explain that we are ALL going deaf at different paces in our lives, almost like a joke.

Once the audiologist finished explaining the test results, he moved on to the treatment for hearing loss. The recommendation was a hearing aid for each ear. Then all the adults sat down and talked with a hearing aid specialist about prices. I had become quite adept at reading upside down to compensate for not hearing what was going on around me. Looking at the invoice, I was able to see the fee for two hearing aids—splish, splash, hearing aids cost lots of cash!

Regardless of the enormous cost, my parents didn't hesitate for even one second. A few weeks later I was fitted for my customized hearing aids at the medical office. As each hearing aid was switched on, I blinked several times. It took a few seconds to figure out what exactly was going on. The volume had been turned up! A new dimension had been added to my world!

At fifteen years old, I could truly hear my mother's voice for the first time. I also heard the sound of the car starting, the wind blowing, and the seatbelt alarm, among other things. Regrettably, this thrill was short lived.

As a teenager, I was mixed up as well as shy. The first day at school wearing my hearing aids was initially exciting, but it quickly turned awkward and embarrassing. My self-conscious tendencies born in grade school were habituated—I still hated being stared at or spoken to because of my shyness and inability to understand speech. As I was dressing for swim class that day, a teammate noticed me removing my hearing aids. She pointed to them, asking me what they were.

As easy as it should have been for me to answer her, it just wasn't. I fumbled with the hearing aids, quickly hiding them in my gym bag. I was unable to respond to my teammate, because I was embarrassed, and ill equipped to answer uncomfortable questions. So I ran off to the pool and started swimming laps. I was so glad to have dodged the question, but I knew I was a coward for avoiding it. As I swam, I thought about what had happened in the dressing room over and over. I knew the question would come up again. It seemed to me that I had two choices:

- Wear the hearing aids and be true to myself.
- Hide the hearing aids and pretend to be something else.

At the end of swim practice, I had made a decision. I chose to be someone else, and I regret that decision like no other. The next day, first thing in the morning, I walked into the girl's restroom and took off my hearing aids for good. Looking back, it's clear that, like many girls my age, I was immature and had very little confidence. And like most other teens, I had made a poor choice, and mine had a lifelong adverse affect. How I wish I'd had the courage to accept myself "as is" and the strength to present myself to others with pride.

My mom would say that it takes more effort to be something that other people want you to be, and much less effort to simply be yourself. My experience tells me that she was right. I would spend year after tiring year trying to be a normal hearing person just like everyone else, something I was never going to be.

When I told my mother that I didn't want to wear my hearing aids for personal reasons, she was dismayed. My version of the truth was like a chocolate-coated pretzel, all twisted up and sugar coated. Though my mother knew there was more to the story, she also knew how shy and self-conscious I was. Instead of a long angry lecture or being grounded for the rest of my life, my mother expressed her disappointment with my decision. She also shared her sadness that I would no longer be able to hear the sounds of the world. I didn't let on at the time, but her words made me think. Perhaps I was missing out on something special. Quickly enough, though, I dismissed the idea of reconsidering.

Near the end of my sophomore year, I developed a relationship with the first real friend of my life—Shelly. Having met her on the swim team, we had several things in common to talk about and experiences we'd shared together. Shelly and I laughed hard, swam hard, and began sharing secrets. This was a wonderful new mystery unfolding, exhilarating because I'd never had the courage or social skills to build a real relationship.

Shelly and I wrote each other notes during classes, handing them off to one other as we passed in the hallway. Communicating with her on the telephone wasn't easy, but we called each other frequently. I didn't express myself in the same way as I did during our face-to-face conversations. On the telephone, I was much more insecure, laughing nervously and pretending to follow what she was saying. But Shelly didn't notice, or she didn't mind, my eccentricity; and our friendship flourished quickly and intensely.

Later on that year, Shelly invited me to spend the night at her house for the first time. I was so excited that I didn't sleep at all the night before. But with the excitement, there was worry. My mother's words came back to me ... disappointment that I would no longer be able to hear the sounds of the world. At Shelly's house, the sounds of the world would be the voices of my best friend and her parents. I feared losing her if the sleepover went badly. What would her parents think of me if I didn't respond to them? How would Shelly feel if I unknowingly treated them rudely? I didn't think I would ever hear from her again.

It was time to make a new decision. I decided that having a real friend for the first time was worth giving my hearing aids another try. In my heart, I knew Shelly was worth it. After I packed my overnight bag, I dug out the hearing aids from my dresser drawer, removed them from their little storage boxes, and looked at them hopefully. Then I placed them in my ears.

These little devices would play such an important role that night. They would be the difference between hearing and not hearing, politeness and rudeness, connection and isolation, acceptance and rejection. This decision was a profound step forward into my excitement for the future instead of leaning backward into the comfort of the past.

Flipping the hearing aid switch to "On" was a positive note, reminding me how gratifying it felt to hear so well! Connecting to the world around me felt good! When my mother dropped me off at Shelly's house, we both had smiles on our faces. I think my mother was happy that I was hearing once again and that I had found a new friend to spend time with. Mothers know how critical it is for teenage girls to share their lives with girlfriends, especially in high school when teens break away from their parents. As we said our goodbyes, we both had so much love in our hearts and high hopes for the night ahead.

My introduction to Shelly's parents went smoothly, and then Shelly and I went to her room to talk. She spoke in a voice that I found soothing and not at all stressful. As a bonus, she almost always spoke to my face and enunciated her words clearly. Of course there is no correct way to pronounce laughter, and maybe that's why we laughed so much. No sooner had the hellos ended than the comical hysteria ensued.

When Shelly's mother called us for dinner, everyone filed into the kitchen. Her mother, father, and brother strolled in first, then Shelly and then me. As we all sat down together for dinner, I hoped. What I was hoping for, I was not so sure, but I hoped for something good and I wasn't thinking about food.

Dinnertime was like a snappy game show with several rewards: learning about each other's backgrounds, sharing stories, and lots of laughter. I had to work hard! Most important, relationships were being built. Shelly and I laughed so hard that we had tears in our eyes. I'm sure her parents must have felt like they were at a carnival but they seemed to appreciate our joyful spirits.

After dinner, Shelly and I decided to watch some television—all the laughing had worn us out, and we were ready to sit back and relax. The living room had two matching recliners so we could both plop down in our own soft chair. We tried our very best to avoid looking at each other, knowing we would likely break out into hysterics once again.

I squirmed in my seat, looking for a comfortable position to relax, but my hearing aids felt like rocks behind my ears. I had to position my head just right, leaning back and looking straight ahead to keep the hearing aids from putting pressure behind my ears.

When Shelly spoke to me, I didn't hear what she said so I turned to face her. As I tried to read her lips, I immediately felt a piercing pressure behind my right ear from my hearing aid. Ouch! I sprang forward, stiffening my body upright and away from the recliner. After our conversation ended, we went back to staring at the television. Shortly thereafter, it happened again—I sprang up, turning toward Shelly to finish the conversation without the hearing aid pinching me.

It was getting late, and we were exhausted. I took off my hearing aids, placing them near my leg. Just a short time later, I opened my eyes to the sound of Shelly's mom asking us something. I had no idea what she said, but Shelly had a happy look on her face and jumped up from her recliner. I decided whatever it was must be good so I jumped up and followed her into the kitchen. As we left the room, Shelly's brother came in and sat in the same recliner I had just walked away from.

At the kitchen table, which seemed to be where all the fun usually began, the three of us happily ate dessert. As we finished up, Shelly's brother walked into the kitchen with a baffled look on his face, holding something up in his hand. I didn't hear what he was saying.

I did what I hadn't done all evening, something I had vowed not to do for the entire sleepover: I ignored him because I didn't hear him. Shelly and her mother stood up to get a better look at the item in his hand. Shelly's mom took it, looked at it closely, then returned it to him as I sat in my chair wondering what all the fuss was about. I had been enjoying my new friends and was in a slight haze, not paying close attention to what was going on around me.

Shelly's brother turned the thing over and around, inspecting it like a dead frog about to be dissected. "What is this thing?" he asked as he crinkled up his nose. Suddenly, I understood that I should be nervous about something.

Opening my eyes wide, I zoomed in on what Shelly's brother was holding in his hand. It was a hearing aid. I had left them on the recliner! Hot blood rushed to my head.

Dear God, please help me! What am I to do? What am I to say?

Then words just fell out of my mouth like gumballs from a candy machine, "Oh, that's mine. I have another one too. They help me hear."

I calmly took the hearing aid from his hand and walked over to the recliner, looking for the other one. "I left them in this chair," I said, searching between the cushions. "The other one must be here somewhere."

They came over to help, asking to take a closer look at the hearing aid in my hand so they could know exactly what they were looking for. I felt like my heart was out on a platter being inspected, and the mere ten seconds they took to examine it felt like ten excruciating hours. What if they were grossed out? Instead, they went back to searching the carpet, and I dug deeper into the recliner seat. Finally, I found the missing hearing aid.

We all sighed in relief! I marched over to Shelly's room and tucked both of the hearing aids in my overnight bag. I was glad to put them to rest for the evening. Behind me, Shelly asked if I wanted to read before going to sleep. I wondered if she realized now that I was different—imperfect—or worse, disabled. Wishfully, I was hoping she didn't understand what had just taken place—that she and her family had discovered my secret "problem." But I told myself that it didn't matter. What mattered was moving forward in my new friendship.

I nodded my approval, and she smiled and retrieved a stack of Reader's Digest magazines for us to choose from. We climbed into bed and opened our magazines. Shelly commented on something and I stopped reading, staring at her as if to say "please don't make me tell you I can't hear; just tell me what you said one more time." When she did, I read her lips and replied. The unspoken rules of being with a hearing-impaired person were becoming clear for both of us.

We did this a few more times. It was quite frustrating and tiresome to anticipate her comments in order to be ready to hear her, so I pretended to be engrossed in my reading material and hoped that she wouldn't be offended that I was more interested in reading than talking. The truth is I wanted her to be quiet so I wouldn't have to hear—because in fact, I couldn't hear. Not without my hearing aids, which would be too painful to wear with my head lying on a pillow.

If only I had the courage to be honest with Shelly and tell her about my needs! But I had denied my hearing impairment for too long. I didn't know how to work through it with a friend because I had never worked through it with myself. The bedroom turned awkwardly silent. But it didn't last long.

Through the magic of teen spirit, the giggles returned after a few uncomfortable minutes. We were at it again! One short giggle erupted into a volcanic explosion of hysterics, complete with comical faces, funny gestures, and oddball noises in the frenzy of best-friendship. No words were necessary in this moment of glee, which was fueled only by the loving, laughing, smiling faces of teenage girls.

When Shelly and I were all laughed out, we finally fell asleep. The next morning, as I put on my clothes before breakfast, I looked at the box that held my hearing aids. I remembered wearing them at the kitchen table the evening before, when the conversation had come quite easily. I wondered if I could have done well without them. Sitting face to face with everyone at the table made things easier—I was close enough to read lips, and to capture as much of their voices as possible.

But more powerful than the kitchen table conversations were the moments of discomfort, awkwardness, and failure. Those experiences stayed with me, reminding me of how it felt to be different. The fear of being different had shaped my initial decision not to wear the hearing aids in the first place. Now, months later, the same type of situation was unfolding at Shelly's house. I wasn't in a place where I felt comfortable with myself. Nor was I in a world that would understand my needs because I did not fully understand them myself. I simply didn't know what I needed or where I fit in.

I returned to my original decision to put the hearing aids away, thinking it would help me make friends and blend in. For several years, it did. The swim team brought fun and laughter into my life—from adolescent silliness in the water to rollicking rowdiness out of water. I didn't necessarily have to hear very well to have friends on the swim team. They were kind, friendly, and playful— and I was able to reciprocate. Almost normal, but with a secret I was unwilling to claim.

★　★　★

Junior and senior year predictably brought more challenges, emotionally and physically. Many of the issues were created by my refusal to accept that I needed help. I needed my hearing aids. Without realizing how they facilitated relationships, I was isolating myself from teammates and friends. This led to misunderstandings with people I cared about, and with some, total disconnections. Friends became upset with me. Miscommunications were the rule. All along I had no idea I was the problem. I was in my own world, disconnected from theirs because I could not hear conversations unless they were right on top of me. I couldn't tell anyone this and I prayed to God that nobody would ever know besides Shelly. I wanted to fit into their world. I wanted to hear! Pretending to hear might make it true. But it never did come true. Although I could hear them muttering, all meaning was lost. But swimmers are loyal teammates and nobody ever walked away from me. Shelly was still my best friend. I had a small circle of friends who stood by me, determined to pull me back when I pulled away in fear.

★　★　★

"Amazing grace, how sweet the sound"! When school ended my sophomore year, my swimming coach asked me if I wanted a job. I felt normal and equal! He hired me as a lifeguard at a local pool. I could hear the hoots and hollering of good fun, and I was comfortable with my ability to sense danger because I had learned to predict human behavior and foresee potential mishaps. I felt good about that because it was something good that I was able to do without enduring conversations and relationships.

Relationships. They had never been my strong point, although the swim team helped me learn to make jokes and eye contact. Deep down, I knew I would lose touch with my teammates once high school was over because I had been unable to develop strong bonds of friendship. I even felt expendable to my own best friend because she would eventually want more than the person I was.

Despite the precariousness of my friendships, my confidence was bolstered in those years, mostly because of my swimming achievements and my coach, who pushed me further than I ever thought I could go. Academically, I failed a few classes but at least I was succeeding as a swimmer. I also developed a sense of humor, made goals for myself, and began thinking about the future.

My senior year, I made a couple of long-term goals for the first time ever. Barely able to function in the real world, I had never before dreamed of accomplishing anything outside the swim team. I had never considered life outside of swimming until I began work as a lifeguard. At the pool, I discovered a passion for children—loving them and teaching them. Several sessions as a swimming teacher gave birth to my first dreams. By using my own experiences to recognize those who were facing personal challenges, I would help children with their struggles and needs.

Then reality set in. I had serious doubts about whether I knew how to even make my dream happen. I would have to graduate from college, and I wasn't even sure that I would graduate from high school! I needed to get into college if I was going to teach. Near the end of my senior year, it was official. After meeting the requirements for graduation and holding my breath for what seemed like generations, my status as a graduating senior of the class of 1982 was confirmed.

IV. A DO IT YOURSELF PROJECT

Swim in the ocean, smile at the sun—
laugh like a baby, shoot like a gun.
Sing like a record, sail with the wind—
laugh out my sillies, pray for my sins.
I'm a son of a gun, a pistol that's loaded
won't stop till I'm done,
or the world has me folded.

—S. L.

1982

I was college bound! High school life was over and real life was about to begin.

Boys? Yes!

Classes? Of course!

Parties? You know it!

Hearing? Not a chance.

They say that in college you get to be who you are. I decided my freshman year that I would rise to the occasion and be the person I really was: a girl who could not hear well. I was determined to figure out how to get through college while staying true to myself. There was only one possible answer: it was time to start wearing my hearing aids.

This was nonnegotiable. Class sizes at the university were huge by my standards. In fact, even with the benefit of hearing aids and sitting in the front row, sometimes I couldn't hear well enough to take quality notes. After my first failed exam, I went back to my dorm room, sat down on the bed, and cried. Then I raised my head and my heart up to God. What now, Lord? I was angry. Instead of crying, I hit the bed.

"Amazing grace, how sweet the sound".

The sound. The sound … of what?

Then I heard it. The sound, how sweet the sound. It was the sound of a mind that can think. A mind that can think can solve problems!

Suffering must be part of survival.

Failure was not part of my plan.

I began thinking, focusing, and problem solving. I had to be fiercely determined if I was going to pass tests and get a degree just like everyone else. Help arrived one day in the form of a fellow student who struck up a conversation during class. She saw my hearing aids and explained how another student would tape record lectures. Then she helpfully suggested that I could do the same.

A double dose of lectures didn't sound appetizing but neither did going back home to live with my parents after flunking out of school. Soon after the idea was planted in my head, I began recording my class lectures. Only one professor objected, pulling me aside after class to express his uneasiness. He was blunt but truthful: he did not like being recorded, and he suggested that I bring an interpreter to class instead. After explaining that I didn't know sign language, he suggested that I learn it.

"But I'm not deaf." I thought to myself.

I wondered why was he trying to push me out of the hearing world after I had spent years trying to hang on to it. The mere suggestion of learning sign language made me even more determined to make it in the hearing world. I was NOT deaf and didn't feel a part of their culture. Deep down, I didn't truly feel a part of the hearing culture either. I was just out there on my own somewhere, trying to fit in but also looking for my proper place. And the deaf community was not my place to be—because I was not deaf. Yet.

I pushed the thought of going deaf out of my mind—it was just too much to consider. I spent my energy on scraping my way by instead, begging professors to let me retake exams and listening to tape-recorded lectures over and over. Unable to hear my professors on tape much better than I could in the classroom, it ended up as a total waste of time.

Just as I had expected, Shelly and I went our separate ways when she decided to join a sorority our sophomore year. It was an emotional parting but I didn't have the tools to cope in a large social setting. I was an emotional wreck just thinking about it. So I rejected the whole concept and walked away. Shelly likely never understood my true reasons for refusing to participate in Greek activities with her, because I never admitted my struggles. I harbored a secret envy of her, and everyone who had what I lacked: the ability to hear, connect, and thrive. It's what I wanted then and something that I have never stopped hoping for.

Activities such as football games, sorority house parties, and mixers with fraternities were a disappointment, each one beginning with high hopes and excitement, and ending with the realization that although I was surrounded by large numbers of happy people, I was on the outside looking in. Activities of this nature were out of the question for me. This I knew for certain now. I accepted it, but I didn't like it.

That same year, a situation arose that was much more serious than falling out with girlfriends. So serious, in fact, that I called my parents sobbing and begged them to come up to help me. A teacher had noticed me swimming one day and conducted a quick interview after class. I was hired on the spot. He must not have noticed my hearing aids or that I was reading his lips. Over the years, people have said that they would never have known I was hard of hearing if I hadn't told them, because of my lip-reading skills and my ability to articulate. Because I might need to save a person's life, I decided to wear my hearing aids while sitting poolside. I knew they would be destroyed if I went into the water for a rescue, but I decided to wear them anyway because a person's life is worth it.

The first month went well, as most people used the pool to work out and already had sufficient swimming skills. These were swimmers of all ages and sizes, roughly half of them college students and the other half faculty members. My lifeguarding coworker was a few years older than me, and we worked well together. Once or twice a week, he would study in the back room with the door closed. When he was done, we would chat by the pool. "Mike" was very funny, so I took time to read his lips. All was going well, and I was earning decent money.

Two months into my lifeguarding job, as I sat alone watching the pool one day, a swimmer from Lane 3 stopped as he was passing by. He looked at me briefly, and then continued on. A few days later, two more swimmers stopped swimming, looking at me in much the same way before continuing on. Almost every day of the following week, swimmers stopped to look at me briefly as I sat in my chair looking back at them. I could not understand this odd behavior, even after scanning the pool area from left to right and top to bottom, and closely watching every swimmer in the pool, I let it pass.

Then one quiet Friday night, as I observed the swimmers while my coworker studied in the back room, someone burst out of the men's locker room door. The door was pushed open so forcefully, it almost slammed right into my face. It was Mike, and he was screaming at me about something. I couldn't understand him because his voice was too agitated. So I stared at him, just as I did with my first-grade teacher, my fifth-grade teacher, my mom, my dad, and many others. And like all the rest, he became even more upset by my lack of a response.

As he walked into the pool office I noticed that several in the pool had stopped swimming to watch the spectacle. This was a feeling that I had long been familiar with. I desperately searched for clues to provide me with the information I needed in order to understand the situation. But there were no clues to be found—no swimmers in distress, no bodies floating, no smoke, no fire, no one had fallen on the deck, and there were no fights or arguments.

Mike came back out of the office and looked at me with concern. "Didn't you hear the phone?" he asked.

I stared at him, bewildered and silent.

"Are you deaf or something?" he added. "Why didn't you answer the phone, Suzie? It's been ringing off the wall!" Exasperation saturated his usually calm voice.

"I didn't hear it ringing," I told him nervously. His body language told me that he was still very upset and my answer was not acceptable.

"The manager has been calling the pool phone for an hour. There were reports of smoke coming from a building down the street. He finally paged me."

I felt sick to my stomach as I realized that I could have put every swimmer in danger by not being able to hear the phone ringing. It could have been someone calling to tell us that the building was on fire, or there was an electrical problem, or just about anything. I would never have been able to take the call because I couldn't hear it ringing—not even with my hearing aids.

The two of us sat in silence for the remainder of the evening. After work, I went home to my dorm room, dragging my feet up the stairwell, and crawled into bed with my clothes on. The whole world could see me failing through the window near my bed. My roommate was gone but I still wanted to hide. I pulled all the covers over my head and cried, briefly but brutally.

When I was all out of tears, I pulled down the covers and noticed the full moon in my window, along with a few stars sprinkled around it. Many years before, sitting in the driveway of my childhood house, I had claimed the sky full of stars as all of my hopes and dreams. This night, the stars had all but vanished. I prayed that this was a temporary setback—that all my dreams would not disappear before my eyes.

Talking to myself, just as I did in first grade as I was in a closet being spanked, I whispered words of solace to heal my spirit. No longer a song, it was now simply the faint words of a private prayer, spoken in hope.

> *Amazing grace, how sweet the sound,*
> *That saved a wretch like me.*
> *I once was lost, but now I am found,*
> *was blind, but now I see.*

The next day I was called into the pool manager's office, where my lifeguarding days were put to an end—and justifiably so. At nineteen years old, this was the first time I was fired. But it wouldn't be the last. Since I could no longer lifeguard, I started looking for something I could do that would help me redeem myself as a worthy individual who was just as capable as the next person. My father arrived to talk with the pool manager and stood by my side as my boss found me another job in the Recreation Department. But I was given work hours that conflicted with my class schedule, so I started searching the want ads for part-time job openings in the area.

A letter arrived in the mail just a few days after the pool incident. It was a card from my mother. On the front was a huge picture of a smiling sun, flashing a very large set of sparkling white teeth. On the inside of the card were two words: Just Because. Below her signature was another smiley face that she had drawn by hand. The card was perfect. If I really thought about it, there were so many reasons to smile. I received many cards from mom throughout college, but this was one of the most perfectly timed and most meaningful. Like finding a four-leaf clover in a meadow, I never got tired of finding a card in my mailbox.

Soon enough, I found work as a waitress at a local dive bar that catered mostly to locals and some homegrown students. The job required me to wear my hearing aids, which I gladly did. I was no longer able to hear a phone ringing but I could still read lips—and could easily carry a tray of drinks around. Knowing my parents would not be thrilled about this type of work, I only told them I would be waitressing, cleverly leaving out the fact that the business was a bar.

The owner, Spyder as his patrons called him, was kind and soft-spoken. He talked about the history of the place then moved on to job expectations and wages in his pure country dialect. Spyder paid ten cents an hour, with the rest of my income being tips.

I had never been in this kind of situation. Waiting tables was something I had only seen others do. It was a symbol of everything I was afraid of, every mountain I had never climbed, and every door I had never opened. So what if I'd been fired for not hearing a phone? Though it was agonizing, the harder the fall, the higher I wanted to bounce back. So when Spyder offered me the job, I accepted. As I walked out of his office, I had butterflies in my stomach. But this was not the time to doubt myself! Acting as my own cheerleader, I whispered— "I can. I will. I MUST!"

I repeated this over and over, all the way home. The first day of my new job was the best, out of the ten days I worked as a waitress. Everyone was trying to be helpful. Other waitresses allowed me to shadow them to learn about the various systems of drink orders and delivery. I was hyped, full of energy with plenty of smiles for the patrons. I was proud to be doing something that a hearing person could do. I felt equal. I wondered if this is what it felt like to be in "their" world. The excitement was a welcome feeling after the humiliation of what had happened at the university pool.

My tenth day as a waitress, I was knocked off the natural high of the wonderful normalcy I had been experiencing by a very unhappy patron. She was a rude woman who wore too much makeup and, I was told, usually had a few too many drinks. While other bar patrons had been repeating their drink orders for me when I asked them to do so, sometimes even writing them down on a napkin, this particular woman was impatient and angry. When I asked for her drink order for a second time to confirm it, she huffed angrily. She did, however, repeat her order.

Unfortunately I heard her incorrectly, even though I had been reading her lips. And oh my, you would have thought I had tried to pass poison off on her.

"What the hell is this?" she hissed when I delivered the drink.

"Ohhh, I thought you ordered this!" I said quickly and apologized. I bent down to get a closer look while asking her to repeat her order one more time.

Before my first word was out, she cut me off.

"Are you deaf or something?" she spat at me, though I don't think she realized her saliva was traveling through the air. Even though I could barely hear, I heard what she'd said very well.

Calmly, I apologized again, promising to bring her the correct drink right away. She rolled her eyes at me, laughed, and mouthed the word "moron" to her friends sitting at the table with her. How I wish I had not seen that. My patience was waning. This was about emotional survival, and I was getting ready to fight back.

But I wasn't ready for war just yet. I wanted to make this right. Suffering leads to survival. Giving up leads nowhere. I had the bartender quickly pour the drink so I could deliver it promptly. Like a team of warriors, the other waitresses rallied around me. One of them even wrote the name of the cocktail on a napkin for future reference, nonchalantly placing it on my tray.

The drink was poured and ready to be delivered. I smiled at her from the bar as she lifted her nose and sneered, her lip curling up like a snotty ten-year-old's. I continued to smile as I walked to her table. She snickered the whole way, looking at me and laughing to her friends. Then when I arrived at her table, she turned her back and ignored me. Now I was angry.

Smiling coyly, I waited for her to turn and face me.

"It's about time!" she said.

"Oh, is this what you wanted?" I asked kindly, motioning to the tall glass filled with liquor, soda water, and PLENTY of ice sitting atop my delivery tray.

"Well here it is," I said. And then I delivered the drink, allowing it to fall out of my hand and onto her body. Ice-cold liquid poured all over her chest, an ice cube even wedging itself in her bosom as she yelped like a poodle and wiggled out of the chair.

Spyder, who sitting at a corner table with some friends, had witnessed the entire incident. He got up, walked to the back of the bar to his office, and motioned for me to come in. This was it. Truth be told, the "accidental" spill was a great release for me. The disappointment of past failures and the anger from ignorant people had been tossed out with the drink, if only for a brief period. But when the satisfaction wore off, reality set in. I had now been fired from two jobs.

That hurt immensely. Fighting back no longer satisfied me. Now I just wished I could figure everything out. It seemed like nothing would. The harder I tried to be "normal" the further away I realized I actually was from being "normal." Instead I was haunted by profoundly abnormal situations. A few times, I felt like giving up. In those dark moments, I wanted to go home and never leave the safety of my parents' house.

Driving home from class one day, I discovered that in addition to being fired from two jobs and struggling to pass my classes, I was also a safety risk to myself. I was crossing over the train tracks near my apartment when my car stalled. This was the first time it had stalled, although it had some engine issues in the past. I tried starting it a few more times, but nothing happened. Out of the corner of my eye, I saw movement—it was a man waving his arms. He was saying something as he pointed to my left. I didn't even bother trying to hear his voice. Instead I looked to where the man had pointed, and saw only a wall of trees shielding the curve in the train tracks emerged. But my focus was getting the car started. I looked back down at the dashboard, problems solving.

Then I looked back to where the man pointed, my eyes moving to above the wall of trees. About a mile or so out I saw a smoke stack moving slowly in my direction. I watched silently, allowing myself time to process this scene. Then a train emerged from behind the trees. I inhaled sharply, holding it as I watched the train chug along the curve in the tracks. My hands shook as I tried the engine once last time. If it didn't start, I intended to get out and run. But this time, it did start. The motor rumbled back to life and I drove off the tracks, scared and shaking.

★　★　★

As time passed, my incapacities continued to become much more defined. The confidence and personal strength I had gained as a high school swimmer waned. On the outside,

I seemed so normal. On the inside, I felt inferior. After two years of the constant fight to survive the daily toil of university lectures, I was sinking.

Most mornings, I joylessly trudged into class without looking at anyone, sometimes spending the entire class period staring at the instructor in silence. I never contributed to class discussions or offered any kind of critical analysis and I felt more abnormal than ever, stupider than ever, and lonelier than ever.

Was there anyone in the world who couldn't hear like me—but wasn't deaf? The truth of what I was and where I belonged felt like the missing pieces to a puzzle. Who am I? What am I? The questions echoed in my head.

Enthusiasm and friendships slipped away. Discouraged, I didn't stop any of this from happening nor could even muster the energy to care. I was no longer my own cheerleader. Late one evening, I drove up to a mountainside in the hill country surrounding the college and parked my car just off the road. Darkness, it seemed, was my friend. Rolling all the windows down, I hung my head out and sat peacefully under the crescent moon perched among billions of stars.

"What now?" I whispered to the moon, hoping an answer might fall out of the sky and into my heart.

The moon and stars, my constant companions over the years, had no answers for me that night, although I did make an ugly decision that I had been trying not to make. With the moon and stars above me, I decided to quit school. When I went home the next weekend, I broke the news to my parents as quickly as possible. My rationale was simple—I wanted to be in a situation where I could do well, and I was tired of trying to survive at school. Calmly, I explained my new plan: go to work in a bank or other quiet place where I could function with limited hearing while making decent money.

My mom wasted no time in putting me back on track. I expected that she would express her sincerest best wishes and whole-hearted agreement. Instead I received a carefully crafted, persuasive lecture about the new car I had been wanting for a very long time. I could reach that goal, she said, once I graduated. Next, she presented her simple argument against my decision—that I wouldn't make the money I was counting on without a degree. With the finesse of a diplomat, she eventually talked me out of quitting.

★   ★   ★

Many times I would lie in bed at night talking to God, asking Him what to do because I still believed there was an "amazing grace." If He could help a lost man be found, and a blind man see, surely my prayers to learn how to fit in this world could be answered. I thought of the professor who suggested that I learn sign language, but once again I pushed the thought away. I was not deaf. And yet neither was I a hearing person. Again, I wondered, what am I?

I needed to figure it out! And I had to believe that I would figure it out. I can, I will and I must. What other way is there to carry on when the odds are against you? I read somewhere that life is a do-it-yourself project. That was exactly what I knew I had to do. Figure it out myself. And graduate. So on I marched into my classes. Luckily, I was too tired to give up. Another moment of surrender had passed. Another layer of character had solidified.

I attended dances and parties those last two years, making it bearable even though the young men I danced and partied with had no idea I couldn't hear half of anything they said. The music was loud enough to hear and that was good enough for me. All you need at a college party is a drink in your hand and a smile on your face.

I did everything I could to get out of college with a degree, even taking History 101 three times before I was able to pass it. Each class was a ninety-minute lecture and you had to know what was important in order to take quality notes. Having failed to hear many lectures in my twenty-one years, I had gotten by guessing on the main ideas and supporting details in high school. In History 101, I guessed wrong. On my third try in summer school, I got it right, and passed.

During those four years of college, I passed some classes with high grades, namely the field courses where I created projects for elementary school children. I scraped through many classes, letting out a glorious sigh of relief when passing grades came in. I also failed some classes, preparing myself ahead of time to accept the mark and move on. And then there were those classes that I dropped at the last minute to avoid receiving a failing mark on my transcript. Each semester presented me with character-building challenges, self-doubt, problem-solving opportunities, and spiritual renewal.

The honest truth is that my grades were never very good. But once in a while, when I was able to participate in class, I felt so smart. When I was able to hear, I could connect—and learn. When I had opportunities to participate in authentic learning, my mind was actively engaged and I was thinking, analyzing, problem solving, creating, integrating, evaluating. In other words, thriving. I graduated college with a Bachelor of Science in education in May 1986. My parents were very excited and proud. Secretly, I think they were also stunned because I had almost given up many times. But no one was more surprised than me.

The day I received notice that I would get my degree, music exploded in my heart. Spontaneously, I improvised my own version of the song that had always remained in my heart, singing and laughing as I jazzed it up with joyful energy:

> *Amazing grace!*
> *A-a-a-amazing grace!*
> *How sweet how sweet, baby-sweet the sound!*
> *Whoa, that saved, yeah saved, a wretched girl like me!*
> *I once was lost, so lost very lost, but now, hey yeah how I'm found!*
> *Was blind, so blind, but now, oh Lord, now I see.*

★   ★   ★

But it was more than a diploma for me. It was testament of the perseverance I had shown, the challenges I had overcome, and the strengths that I had developed. That all far outweighed the benefits of academic knowledge. This was a fight well fought—and I had won!

After four years of studying, searching, and survival, one haunting question remained: "Where do I fit in this world—with the hearing or the deaf?" It would be another twenty-five years before a series of life-changing events gave me the answer I had been looking for. For now, I preferred to let that question fall away unanswered.

I didn't know where I was going, but I did know that I had to keep putting one foot in front of the other. It was the only way to move forward in the right direction, wherever that was. On a sunny clear afternoon, in May 1986, I focused on that day, graduation day. It was the best day of my life.

V. TWO JOURNEYS, ONE LIFE: TEACHER, LEARNER

Time, commonly referred to as life,

is a one-time gift.

You must live it while alive!

—S.L.

1986

In 1986 I embarked on two journeys, teaching and learning. I had snagged a job as a first-grade teacher. After landing my first job in the field of education, Step 1 was to purchase my first car, one of the motivations that got me through college. It was a small sporty economy model with a fading red stripe across the body, perfect for a young single girl on a budget.

Step 2, I had to get my classroom ready. The first day of school was only three weeks away. This step involved spending money I didn't have on teaching materials. But I needed to fill my empty classroom. The district provided some materials, but not enough to create a rich learning environment. In less than one month's time, my credit card was maxed out, but I had bought enough cute posters, organizers, flashcards, and pencils to fill ten classrooms.

★   ★   ★

The flashcards were sorted and stacked. Colorful laminated posters hung from the walls. The pencils lay bundled and sharpened. My briefcase and lunch box were packed, and I'd even ironed my clothes. The next morning, I began my career as a first-grade teacher. "Inauguration Day" commenced promptly at 7:00 A.M. as I entered my classroom for my very first day of school. I couldn't believe it!

I was hustling around the classroom making last-minute preparations when my very first student walked into class. He was alone. Glancing at the clock, I noticed it was well before school was officially open. A six-year-old child walking around alone that early in the morning was startling. This courageous little fella was dressed in a muscle shirt and torn jeans as he bashfully stepped inside my room. He had one hand in his front pocket and held a lone pencil in the other hand. My first student!

I walked over and kneeled down to his eye level, smiling at him. His grin was shy but confident, and missing one front tooth. This little guy's first words remained locked sweetly in my memory: "Hey, you my teacher?"

As I introduced myself, he looked at me attentively and then spoke again. At that point I discovered my first challenge of the day—understanding him through his thick Spanish accent. I politely asked him to talk a little louder so I could hear him, which patiently he did. It helped a little, but I needed him to repeat himself once more before I was able to capture his entire message:

"I'm in your class. I'm Angel."

"Welcome to first grade, Angel!" I said, and he quickly asked if he could sharpen his pencil. I smiled. He was Angel. I was so happy to be his teacher. I nodded as we walked over to the pencil sharpener. In just over two minutes, I had fallen in love with him.

The rest of the day was filled with even more memorable moments as I became acquainted with the rest of my students. All of my students, and their parents, who walked through the door that day were greeted with a smile and a friendly hello. The children held bags of school supplies while their parents had scores of questions. As my classroom began filling up with children and parents, the noise level increased. Conversation was becoming a challenge but I was too busy to worry about it. Luckily, by 9 A.M. all the parents were out of my classroom. At that point, it was just my little ones and me.

There was a noisy buzz of twenty-two six-year-olds excited to learn. As I began checking in supplies, I noticed that their little voices seemed to be miles away. When students began asking me questions, their faraway voices could not be ignored. This challenge was on the front burner now so I accepted it. Communication between us was slow and straining, but the show had to go on.

By noon, I had a plan. I asked my students to raise their hands when they wanted to speak to me. They would not be required to remain completely silent, which was physically impossible for a six-year-old. Instead, when a student's hand went up in the air, I went flying over to the student's desk and kneeled down so we were face to face. That way, I was able to catch enough of the child's voice to understand the message. For the remainder of the day, the problem was solved. As an added bonus, I must have burned ten thousand calories dashing from desk to desk.

That first day of my teaching career, I fell in love twenty-two times. The beauty I saw in each little set of eyes, each small hand, each diminutive smile and each precious little voice was all the motivation I needed to carry on for the rest of the day, week, year— and for the rest of my life.

With fondness, even after twenty-five years, I still recall Angel's tiny little arms emerging from his muscle shirt, Chris' unbelievably beautiful eyelashes, Jennifer's enthusiasm, Lata's accent, John's inquisitiveness, Eliza's long black hair, Mike's ever present toothless smile, Tommy's wavy blond hair, BJ's bashfulness, Anniemay's honesty, Yvette's giggle, Adam's dimples, Sabrina's shyness, and Jenny's sensitive big brown eyes. I felt honored to have a place in the lives of first-graders who, after only six years of life, had left the comfort of home for a seven-hour marathon of academia—and they did it all without a nap.

I knew it was my place to be with them, this year in particular, their first real year of graded schoolwork, the beginning of an epic twelve-year adventure and maybe the road to a college degree for some. This was the life I was born to live. At the end of that first day, I evaluated my performance. I got my highest grade in preparedness: The flashcards had been perfect. The posters brightened the room. And the pencils were sharpened.

But there was one thing that I couldn't buy at the supply store— the ability to hear. I had never thought about it, but just as I aged, my hearing aids had aged as well. They were archaic and no longer helped me. I needed new ones.

I went straight home to scour the Yellow Pages for hearing aid vendors. That evening I found myself nervously walking into a hearing aid office inside a major department store at a local mall. I prayed that they would have a better hearing aid that would give me a way to communicate effectively with my little ones! I needed amplification to the nth degree. Of all the schoolteachers in America, I had to be the only one wanting to turn the volume up in a classroom instead of down.

Four weeks later, thanks to new hearing aids that were impressively powerful, I could hear the little voices of my first-graders in much more detail and volume. Combined with lip reading and close physical proximity to my students, the communication gap was considerably narrowed. Certain things would continue to pose problems, such as hearing speakers at faculty meetings or staff development courses. But I was thankful that the most important voices were being heard—the voices of my children.

The first few years of teaching were passed quickly. I was learning the ropes right along with my students. There were a few kids I didn't want to let go of when the day ended—and so I didn't. Those kids were lovely souls and in some cases, they had the parents to match. With parental permission, I occasionally took them bowling or to a movie. Of course I wasn't able to follow the storyline of the movie, but it didn't matter. I was living the life I had always wanted to live, with children and for children. It was grace of the most amazing kind and I was thankful for it.

Conscious of the many professional obligations for teacher development, I attended training workshops with my colleagues. One session after another was wasted on me because I could not participate. I always walked purposefully to the front row, taking the best spot to read the presenter's lips from. But again and again, I couldn't hear well enough to benefit from the information covered. Minutes, hours, whole days of staring at a speaker passed without a speck of understanding. The amount of work it took to hear a single sentence rapidly was staggering, always sapping my energy level and enthusiasm.

At one particular training session, several speakers were constantly interjecting to support or add to each other's points, and I was worn out after only an hour into the workshop. From what I had read about the speakers beforehand, I knew this was a top-quality workshop. They were nationally known for their expertise and their sense of humor. I sat silently watching the people around me, who were completely enthralled, completely still except for their blinking eyes. At times, the entire audience broke out into laughter, agitating me further. It felt unreal and unfair, a consequence of my physical limitation that I could do nothing to fix. I had new hearing aids, I was sitting in the front row, and I was reading lips—but I still couldn't follow. Locked out of the hearing world again with nowhere else to go. I wasn't deaf. But I couldn't hear. Who was I?

At one seminar, realizing that I would spend my entire day sitting in a chair trying to do the physically impossible once again, I sighed heavily and put my pen away. Staring at the blank sheet of notebook paper that seemed to mock me with its emptiness, I wondered what to do. Something or nothing? I had had enough of the existing situation so I decided to do something to change it. From my seat, I began to think. It was time to problem solve.

I needed an action plan. My initial plan was to go home. That's what I really wanted to do. It hurt my feelings and ego that a teacher as excited to learn as I was would be shut out of learning. It was halting my professional development, holding me hostage to the status quo. I wanted grow! How could I fix this? My hearing aids provided limited benefit in large settings, so that was that. It seemed as if the case was closed.

Looking around the room, I studied the eager faces, the bored faces, the sleepy faces—and I thought about the face I had on: the fake face. I was wearing the face of a pretender. For hours, it seemed, I had been sitting there pretending to be engaged in the seminar. I was angry with myself for considering leaving instead of coming up with a better solution. Then I turned my anger on the situation itself and became defiant, deciding that I would not be shut out of professional development. It was time to fight again.

So from that moment on, each time I became worn out by reading lips through squinted eyes, my action plan was to get up, walk out of the auditorium, and go for a drink of water. I would return with energy stored up for another round of fighting for my place in education. I was fighting for my place in life. I was determined that yes, I could, and yes, I would—because I had to.

The plan worked, and I did benefit that day to the extent that my lip-reading skills compensated for my inability to hear actual voices. It was exhausting, but it was the only solution I had come up with, and it worked. Once again, His amazing grace had provided what I needed. For that I had to be thankful—imperfect blessings are still blessings. Imperfect people are still people.

★   ★   ★

One of the amazing powers of grace is its positive energy. It's powerful enough to lead you out of darkness and into the light, strong enough to pick up the spirits of those who are sinking, filling them with lightness and beauty through all the days of their lives. What I had dubbed my strong song, "Amazing Grace", gave me strength in moments of desperate isolation.

I began to hear the voice of strength speaking to me when I had doubts and fears. This voice—my voice—repeated the same thing over and over like a broken record.

> *I can. I will. I must.*
> *I can. I will. I must.*
> *I can. I will. I must.*

It didn't sound like my normal voice, more like I was tapping into some energetic force. Perhaps it was the power of "Amazing Grace" that had been leading me through hardships and was now steering me through rougher waters. However it worked, this mantra shifted my focus from giving up to moving forward and carrying on, one step at a time.

To this day, when faced with an impossible task, I center myself with this "can do" mantra—a powerful force in my own voice that had been placed in my head by "Amazing Grace." It carried me through the first few years of my career in education when I could not find a way to fit into a world where hearing was necessary but impossible, and it helps me now.

During those first few years of teaching, I discovered many other challenges in my classroom that had nothing to do with my hearing impairment. Each student had his or her own personal challenge that led to self-doubt, fear, and anxiety. Picking up their needs to have their own coping mechanisms, I introduced my Can Do mantra to the class. I made the signs and hung them on the walls: I CAN. I WILL. I MUST. Would it work?

I couldn't be sure, but my time as a teacher had taught me that even six-year-old children can learn how to be positive, to believe they can overcome—and then overcome. Unfortunately, my Can Do mantra might have been the only encouragement that some of them heard all day. They worked together to overcome different issues, never going into detail about the struggles of one another but collectively supporting each other with highly enthusiastic comments such as "Yes, you can! You will! And you must!"

Outside of school, I was growing both as a young teacher, and as a young woman. I began spending time with my mother, now seeing her as a friend as well as a mom. It was important to me that she knew I was making it on my own. I took her to lunch or dinner a few times a month, always sharing my classroom experiences with her. My mother and I had great fun and conversations chewing the fat, as they say, over dinner. When I married at twenty-eight, we had even more great conversations because now we had something in common—we were both married women.

As close as we were becoming, I never made mention of my scrambles for a solution when I could not hear. Those I kept hidden from her. Rather than complain, it was more important that I spend the energy finding ways to survive. I had learned to distance myself from complainers and did not wish to become one. So I didn't tell my mother when:

- I could no longer hear my cat's meow clearly—and then one day I realized it had disappeared altogether.
- Music coming from my car stereo began fading away, even when I turned the volume all the way up.
- Attending church had lost its appeal because there were simply too many people talking over one another at Sunday school for me to follow the discussion. I didn't feel safe enough to join in, so I simply stopped going.
- In addition to Sunday school, the church message itself was lost in the echoes of the sanctuary.
- I couldn't have lunch with friends after the service was over because I couldn't function in large groups or in large, noisy restaurants. I became disconnected from my Sunday school singles group.
- The voices of passengers riding in my car with me were muffled and faded, making it very nearly impossible to converse with them. I was forced to listen as hard as I could, process what little I could hear, and when I simply couldn't understand what they were saying, fake my way through my half of the conversation. I refused to admit that I was inching my way to deafness. Instead I was sure I could figure out verbal exchanges with a few more bits and pieces. But it never happened that way.
- The telephone ringing sounded farther and farther away, even on the loudest setting.
- I was unable to pick up most of the music at my wedding even with my hearing aids, including a live rendition of

Pachelbel's Canon in D Major by a flutist I had picked.

- The doorbell to the first house I ever owned appeared to be broken, until I was told that, in fact, it did work. It was my ears that were broken.

- And I didn't tell my mother that her voice on the telephone was becoming quite difficult to decipher, even when she spoke louder. The gibberish I was hearing required me to do an enormous amount of guesswork during most of our conversations. It was exhausting.

★　★　★

All of these hindrances were irritating, but not life threatening. The nightly news humbled me with pictures of tragedy, sadness, pain, and violence. But in the warm safety of a classroom full of children learning to read and write, there was other news. There was hope.

Hope put things into perspective. Amid all the pain and suffering in the world, there was also amazing grace in the form of a baby bundled up in its mama's arms, the sun coming up over the horizon, a child skipping in the street, and a classroom full of little ones telling me that I looked beautiful on my worst hair day ever. That was amazing grace. It was the beautiful feeling of being grateful for my blessings; it was the music of "Amazing Grace", the song I had been singing in my heart through the ups and downs on the fringes of the hearing world.

One Saturday morning, my mom discovered how meager my hearing was when she called to say hello. Instead a chat, we went on an emotional rollercoaster ride. I never wanted anyone, especially Mom, to experience the intense highs and lows that were the hallmark of my life. But that morning, she did.

My husband told me that the cellphone was ringing so I sprang out of bed to answer the call before whoever it was hung up. I could only assume it was family since I rarely gave out my number. It was a painful process when someone new called, and I often simply hung up after hearing only fragments of what the person was saying. I knew that if it was important call, they would call back and I would let it go to voicemail, which I could listen to on speakerphone. But I was familiar with the voices of my immediate family and able to fill in the blanks of what I could not hear. This time, I took the call but there was no one on the other end, so I hung up. I kept the phone in my hand, waiting to see whether they would call back. A few seconds later, the screen lit up.

"Hello?" I said.

There was a very weak, faint noise. I couldn't determine whether it was a male or female—it sounded like someone breathing heavily or wind blowing into the microphone. It sounded very different than an unclear voice, so instead of hanging up, I stayed on the line, listening carefully to the unusual noise and pressing the phone to my ear as tightly as I could.

I caught part of a phrase sounding like a very distraught, "Suzie, this is Momma." If it was my mom, then she was crying intensely, unable to speak. The sound of wind blowing suggested that she was hyperventilating. These thoughts frightened me as I continued to listen, trying to identify who it was and what they wanted. Soon I was panic-stricken. I decided that it was my mom, and she was crying because of some terrible accident had happened.

"Momma? Momma?" I tried to say more but those were the only words that would come out. My heart felt as if it had stopped. I was about to suffocate yet breathing rapidly.

"Momma, what's wrong, what is it?" I called out to her in anguish. Her voice became more bizarre and sounded like she was even more distressed than she had been. I was completely unable to move as the tears were pouring out of my eyes. I was certain that something very, very bad had happened and someone was hurt—or dead.

It was no use trying to figure this out so I gave up, handing the phone over to my husband. Overcome, I fell out of bed and down on my knees, crying with my head buried in my hands. I couldn't breathe, and my mind was distraught. My husband spoke briefly, and listened. Quickly, he put the phone down and rushed over to me, saying, "Everything is okay. Everyone is okay. Your mom was sick and lost her voice. Everything and everyone is okay."

He must have repeated himself ten times while I stared into the nothingness of shock, letting it sink in. When I finally looked at him, he added, "She just called to say hello, that's all."

That's all. A call to say hello. That's all it took to change my life forever. After that, the sight of a cell phone lighting up or ringing made me jumpy, nervous, panicky, and sometimes even sick. It didn't last, however, because a few short years later I became totally deaf to the sound of any ringing phone.

VI. TWO MORE FEET

Your little eyes, full of surprise, reflect the way I feel today.

To see you play, and run my way, it seems you came just yesterday ...

The doctor smiled, inspected you awhile, then let your dad hold his little lad.

Your daddy cried, and then he sighed, "Can't you see he looks like me?"

Then at last, your daddy passed your bundled body to your new mommy.

Of course, I cried—and then I tried to wake you with a gentle kiss.

I held you close, all night or most, 'til dawn delivered morning sun.

Your sleepy eyes, they opened wide,

gazed up above, and I fell in love.

Since that day I cannot say I'd live my life another way.

You are my son, till the world is done.

'Til kingdom come, you are my son.

— S. L.

1995

The key words of 1995 were education, emotion, excitement, and evolution. In my heart, I'd held onto the dream that being a mother wouldn't require excellent hearing, only the ability to love. I felt fortunate to have been born with the gift of unending patience and deep love for small children. It was a love so powerful that all of my students felt like my own. If I ever was to be blessed with the gift of a little baby, I was ready to love my child with all my heart and care for him with every bit of energy my body could offer, hoping that this would compensate for whatever inconveniences my hearing loss would cause.

On August 26, 1995, shortly after my thirtieth birthday, our firstborn child arrived; a beautiful little boy. We named him Conner. And it was the best day of my life. Everything was ready for him when we came home from the hospital. I had read all the books in anticipation of the big moment, and my husband and I had worked all summer long to have his room properly decorated and equipped. I had been preparing all my life to love a warm little person. This was the culmination of all the experiences of my journey into adulthood. This was motherhood.

I was so happy that first night at home with my little baby boy! Tears of joy steadily trickled down my cheeks the entire night as I gazed at his perfect little profile sleeping in my arms. It was so perfect,

77

so peaceful, so quiet. I wondered if this was the sound of love. In that moment, I didn't allow myself any negative thoughts about being a hearing-disabled mother. How could there be anything bad about motherhood when this kind of beauty existed in the world?

The first few weeks as a new mother were probably the easiest. The toughest challenge was overcoming a lack of sleep but my husband was a doting dad, always ready to spend time with his baby boy while I rested. And the adrenalin rush of first time motherhood offset some of the fatigue, so I didn't feel as worn out as I looked. As any mother knows, newborns do three things: eat, sleep, and produce dirty diapers. I was happily very proficient at fulfilling my son's daily need for liquid food, a warm, safe place to sleep, and a clean, dry diaper.

The first sign of trouble began when I turned on the baby monitor. It didn't work. Before our son was born, my husband and I practiced using the monitor system by talking into the transmitter like a walkie-talkie, then determining our preferred volume setting on the receiver. While I spoke into the transmitter from the nursery, my husband was able to hear my voice with the volume set on three. Lights flashed across the screen, matching the intensity of the sound—the louder the voice, the more lights on the screen. Then we switched places and he spoke into the transmitter while I listened to the monitor from another room. My preferred volume setting was six out of the maximum of ten. As red lights flashed while he spoke into the transmitter, I moved the volume to number ten, curious of the outcome. The high volume distorted the sound, creating little more than garbled static. When my husband and I discussed the results of our little test, I didn't mention to him that, though I could hear his voice, his words were incomprehensible.

But that didn't really matter, did it? A newborn baby wouldn't be doing any talking! All that really mattered was that I heard some sort of sound coming from the monitor; since it could only be my baby's cry. When the time came to use the monitor system, the transmitter would sit atop my baby's changing table in his nursery. The receiver would go wherever I went throughout the house. That was the plan, although we didn't need it those first weeks when our baby boy slept in a bedside bassinet.

Much was done to prepare for Conner's journey to his crib in the nursery. But things didn't go as I had planned. I discovered on his first night in the crib that the monitor was going pick up a lot more than his crying. When one to two lights were blinking, we determined that the transmitter was picking up inconsequential sounds. I began calling these sounds "odds and ends" because they were sounds of things around the house such as: a door closing, the vacuum cleaner, a lawnmower outdoors, the air conditioner clicking. As each sound came through, I got up and walked to the nursery, not knowing whether our son was fine until I checked his crib and found a sleeping baby.

I wasn't concerned by the false alarms. What did concern me, however, was my inability to hear my baby's actual cries. When there were five, six, seven, even eight little red lights racing across the face of the device, I had expected to hear something. I was alarmed because these little red lights were the actual cries of my baby boy! I could hear Conner's cries when I held him—but I couldn't hear any part of his cries through the monitor. This made no sense. Why wasn't I able to hear his voice on the monitor as he cried?

The more it happened, the more I had to think about it, and a sick feeling crept into my heart. Realizing I had to use his actual cries to register on the monitor, I would wait for naptime, when I knew he would object—and cry. I finished my normal routine of feeding him, changing him, and snuggling as he fell asleep in my arms. Then I laid him down in his crib and closed the door. In the hallway, I leaned on a large pillow, waiting for his cries to help me figure out what was going on. In a few hours' time, he was set to awaken, and his cries were certain to set the little red lights aglow.

And they did. The lights began flickering, first two, then four, five, six, and eight lights, matching the pattern of his anxious cries. Quickly, I took the monitor and placed it close to my ear. On volume level six, I could barely detect the cry, if that's what I was hearing at all. I moved the dial up to seven, keeping the monitor pressed against my ear. The muffled sound was a bit louder. As I removed the monitor from my ear, the sound faded completely out. I nudged the dial up to level eight, holding the monitor a few inches from my ear. I heard something!

I bumped the volume up to number nine. Yes! My son was crying! And I heard it! His cries weren't normally something that I hoped to hear, but this time I was happy and relieved. My baby was crying and he needed me. Of this I was absolutely certain, but I had to act fast. I needed to see and hear him crying simultaneously to confirm that what I heard coming from the monitor were his actual cries. Anxiously, I pushed open his door. My baby boy, distressed and impatient, greeted me with an edgy grunt, as if to say, "What took you so long, momma? I'm hungry!"

His cries never sounded better than they did that afternoon, except maybe the night he was born when he cried so loudly that the doctor proclaimed his lungs to be in fine shape. I was relieved to have removed another obstacle challenging my right to motherhood. Though I didn't like to think about it, my hearing impairment was closing in on me. This disability was stealing my liberties.

I faced each day after that one with an action plan in place, ready to face the Monitor Challenge head on. The receiver sat on the edge of my night table, a few inches away from my pillow. The volume was set on number nine. Between the sound and the lights, I was sure to awaken and tend to the little baby boy at the other end—at least for a while.

My husband had been kind enough to work with me through all these issues and patient enough to help me hear when I could not. I knew I was lucky to have been blessed with an understanding spouse, and I truly believed that most people in the world also had kind, loving hearts. Unfortunately, I didn't realize how far removed some people were in their understanding of hearing impairment or deafness until I had an actual taste of it a short time later.

A friend of my husband came over for an after-work visit. He was a pleasant enough person with a lovely wife who stayed home to care for their small son. The two of them sat at the kitchen bar talking as I prepared dinner. Feeling no pressure to follow their conversation, I had a silent one-way conversation with myself, as I always did during solitary tasks.

Not until years later was I told that the conversations I had with myself were not silent at all. I had been uttering words, phrases, and sentences that were loud enough to be heard by everyone— except me. To strangers, I appeared to have an imaginary friend. To my friends and family, my behavior seemed normal.

We had a small television on the kitchen counter to provide me with a talking head to look at when I tired of my own chitchat. I chopped tomatoes and shredded lettuce, glancing occasionally at the television to read the captions on the evening newscast. A weather report caught the attention of the men seated at the bar. Then my husband's friend barked, "What the hell is that?" It was an ugly, angry, abrasive remark.

"What are you talking about?" my husband and I asked in unison.

His reply was agitated and impatient. "Those word things in the box, right there at the bottom of your TV! What are they?!"

My gut reaction was sadness. I felt rejected. But I kept a stiff upper lip and replied calmly. "Oh, that's captioning. It's so you can read what they're saying."

I wasn't sure what surprised me more, his obnoxious reaction or that he had never seen closed captioning before. I was determined to help him learn something about my world, so I delivered an impromptu public service announcement about the challenges faced by the deaf and hearing-impaired community. He stared as if he couldn't understand a word I had said, so I repeated myself in a different way.

After explaining what closed captions were a second time, and the gift that captioning offered to the deaf community, he launched into an expletive-filled tirade, ranting on and on about how irksome and annoying the words moving along the bottom of the screen were to him.

My husband and I were stunned. Neither one of us could fathom how a person could be so astonishingly self-centered and insensitive. I was silenced. And humiliated beyond the boundaries of anything I had ever faced. I had never experienced such a personal and vicious attack on the hard of hearing or disabled. I briefly felt sorry for myself, but in the long run I felt sorrier for him.

The challenges I had been facing all my life as a hearing-impaired person actually strengthened and prepared me for these callous, thoughtless comments. Digging deep for every bit of fortitude I could possibly find, I let my spirit take the lead and moved past his hurtful remarks. But the incident diminished the collateral of pride that I had been gleaning all those years, all of my life.

I would establish a bulwark of pride, and then lose it. Obtain it again, only to lose it again in a seemingly never-ending cycle. I wondered whether life was this difficult for everyone, or if God had made a mistake when He made me.

It didn't matter. Surviving mattered. I had endured for thirty-five years, and I knew there was nothing to do but continue on. In the bleakest of moments, a fighting spirit would always rise from the ashes of my burned-out heart. This was one of those moments. I was at the end of my rope—but not the end of my hope.

After my husband's friend left that evening, I quietly went about my business, cleaning up, preparing schoolwork, taking care of my baby boy, and fighting off the demons that were telling me I was unworthy. I continued singing my strong song, "Amazing Grace", during the tough times—in my heart, in my head, in my car, and in the shower. Sometimes silently, other times as loud as my heart and lungs could sing. The song helped me stay aware that my challenges could also be my successes, once I overcame them. Obstacles to me hearing were popping up all over, and I needed something to pick me up each time. "Amazing Grace" always came through.

★　★　★

The school cafeteria had become a source of misery for me, with its head pounding noise and controlled chaos. Teachers were responsible for watching the kids—not an easy task for anyone, but much more difficult without the ability to hear. I didn't bother to turn up the volume on my hearing aids—they were simply of no value because of the intensity of sound and the number of kids speaking at once. If anything, I would have preferred to turn the volume down—I didn't want to hear noise, I wanted to hear voices. Up until then, I had been capturing scattered pieces of student voices in the cafeteria. And despite the overall effect being less than desirable, it was tolerable because I could at least partially understand.

But no longer. My world was changing, and the evidence was clear—my hearing had deteriorated to a new low. It didn't matter how close I stood to a student, or how high I turned up my hearing aids. Voices were unintelligible in situations with loud background noise. I had to completely rely on lip reading.

It was almost more work than humanly possible, in a cafeteria filled with eighty kids. But once again through fancy footwork, I ran up and down the aisles to read the kids' lips, just as I had my first year of teaching when my hearing aids didn't work. Even more draining was the task of concealing my actions from my colleagues. Incredibly, I was still hiding my hearing impairment because I didn't want to be disabled , and I didn't want help. I wanted to make it in their world—because I didn't know where else to go.

I wanted to hear. Month by month, the children and I made it work, somehow. I was born to teach. I was born to live a life of purpose and determination, and to offer my students the same. By striving to succeed, I was teaching determination by living it, even if the details of my struggle remained private.

A turn of events in 1997 eliminated the stresses and helped overcome some obstacles. My husband was transferred to another city, requiring us to relocate a few hours away. Immediately, I set up interviews with several principals. All the interviews went well, but one interview went exceptionally well. So well, in fact, that it offered me a new direction with more professional development, fewer physical demands, and the chance to work with children in a small-group setting. In my new capacity as a reading specialist, I would conduct one-on-one reading lessons in the morning, for thirty minutes at a time.

Then I would provide reading assistance to older children in small groups.

Now that Conner was two years old, I no longer wanted to be working in my classroom every weekend or bringing home a satchel full of papers to grade each evening. I wanted to be a mommy when I was finished being a teacher at the end of the workday. This new opportunity couldn't have come at a better time. Perhaps I had found a place in this world where I could truly fit in and gain control of my circumstances. I settled into a portable building with one other reading specialist who had the same schedule as mine. The room was always quiet—the perfect environment to do my best teaching, and conducive to learning as well. This was what I had needed for a very long time.

Also that year, I began taking my son to the neighborhood swimming pool. Now that he was two, I guessed that he might enjoy swimming very much. How exciting that I might pass on a few swimming skills to my son. I would have to remove my hearing aids, but I could read his lips with relative ease because he didn't speak in complete sentences yet.

On our first few dips into the big blue water at the pool, Conner and I spent most of the time giggling and splashing. We were having so much fun! It didn't matter that I couldn't hear his giggling or that my eyeglasses were covered in water drops. His ear-to-ear smile connected us heart to heart.

The next time we went to the pool, I left my glasses in my gym bag. How could I have not foreseen the consequences of removing my glasses, when I was dependent on my eyes to hear? Almost as soon as we stepped into the water, I realized that this would not be how I had imagined it. Our fun day at the pool came to a dead end the minute he stopped giggling and began talking to me. His dad held him a few feet away from me, yet I heard only faraway crackles of sound. I searched for his joyful eyes and moving mouth, but saw only a blur of face and hair.

I couldn't hear my boy's voice. I couldn't read his lips either. Moving closer in, I hoped to capture his voice. By the time I could finally decipher his voice, I was right in his face—not the interaction he wanted. He wanted me to play with him, splash with him, and communicate with him. I had to fix this. I was determined to play with my son in the swimming pool. This was one of the things I had been waiting to do all my life and one of the little rewards for working hard as a parent. These potentially happy moments required solid communication between mother and son.

I got out of the pool and rushed to my bag, removed a beach towel, and dabbed the dripping water from my hair and face, then put in my hearing aids. Then I took a deep breath—not to release the stress over possibly damaging my hearing aids. No, it was a deep breath full of hope that I would be able to participate in this special moment with my son. I said a quick prayer: "Please, God, let me in. Let me into this moment."

Entering the water gracefully, to avoid any splashes, I motioned to my husband that I was wearing my hearing aids. He looked surprised. I waded over, stopping about three feet short of them, far enough away so that they wouldn't splash my hearing aids. I accepted that I wouldn't be able to hold my boy in return for being able to hear and interact with him from a safe, dry distance.

His first and natural response was to splash me. My first and natural response was to frown at him because my hearing aids were getting wet. Anxiety was building …if only he could understand—I didn't want to splash with him, I wanted to communicate with him. He splashed again. I frowned again. My husband, seeing frustration written all over my face, suggested that we all play in the back yard later, as a gentle offering to me. He had tried for years to help me deal with my growing disability, dependency, and frustration but all he could do was watch me struggle, offer support, and hope I figured it all out.

Before I could answer, something splashed me from behind. I spun around to see a little boy in his mother's arms doing precisely what little boys do in the water—he was splashing. Then I looked back at my own son who continued to giggle with my husband. It was a tense moment. Resentment briefly crept into my heart toward the other mom who could hear her son's laughter. But it fell away quietly as I realized they weren't to blame for my frustrations. I was upset, confused, and sad. Then a different kind of darkness set it. I was heartbroken.

As I climbed out of the pool, I watched the blur of Conner his daddy's arms, yet heard nothing. Distraught, I tried to accept that I had been cut out of a special moment in my son's life. Accept it and move on, I repeated.

I can accept this, I said to myself, zoning out of the world.
I will accept it, because I must accept it.
And I tried my best to believe it. But I just couldn't.

The pill was bitter. My private mantra went round and round in my head—I can, I will, I must—but it didn't lift me up this time. Hoping to sing myself to acceptance, I started with my strong song. "Amazing Grace", I sang weakly—then stopped. I didn't see or feel any amazing grace. How was singing going to help me? What purpose could there be for my inability to communicate with my child?

I didn't fit in this world. Why was I trying to belong here? Why had I been put here, where I obviously didn't belong, in the first place? My backbone crumbled as I faced the slimy monster of self-pity. And then from somewhere deep inside myself, I drew upon the most powerful weapon I had: faith. Walk by faith, not by sight.

After a few moments wrapped in the warm cloak of faith and I knew why I was here, in a world where I didn't fit in, and why I would continue trying. Because this was where my son lived. This was where my husband lived. This was where my family lived. My friends. My job is. This was my life.

And besides, if not here, then where? There was no other place that could possibly be for me. How I wished I could understand this madness. I didn't know how much spunk I had left, and I was tired of fighting for my place in the world.

VII. LITTLE BIT AND NONNER

Like a hand-painted canvas, he stood tall in the ballpark.

Oh, this radiant diamond was a true work of art.

He stepped up to bat, looking larger than life,

knowing the pitch would cut like a knife.

As he held up his chin, then steadied his grip,

he pulled his arms back and stared down the pitch.

Just who was this player? Who stood by home plate?

Who looked so familiar, who made my heart race?

A babe at one time, a toddler no more, the young man I saw

was my very own newborn twelve years before.

This is a moment etched in my heart,

~the gift of my son~

God's work of art..

—S.L.

1998

On September 9, 1998, at 8:42 P.M., my second son was born. Randy's birth was a joyful event, with all the marvel and magic that comes with the arrival of a new little bundle of love. It was the best day of my life, even as I saw my marriage unraveling due to the complications and tensions of life.

"Little Bit," as we came to call him, was born happy, giggling for the first time at only three days old. There was a long list of things that made my newest little boy smile. One of his favorites was to simply stare at big brother Conner, who was now three years old. As a newborn, Little Bit would sit in his bouncer seat smiling at me as I prepared dinner, or folded clothes. Meanwhile, Conner went about his playful ways of pushing cars around, stacking blocks, and taking toys apart.

Little Bit loved the entertainment his big brother provided— the various movements, colors, and sounds. My two boys were not yet communicating verbally, and I enjoyed sitting back and just watching, not needing to hear anything at all. We entertained one another and grew close together as the days passed, almost as if an invisible thread attached us, drawing us tighter and tighter together with each kiss, hug, or smile. Our loving connection during that time was a declaration of the power of nonverbal communication. Hearing was not a requirement to snuggle or smile, and those were the best days of my life.

Those two boys were my number one focus, my heart, my life. I spent my daytime hours working to give my students the same kind of education I hoped my sons would receive, and the rest of my day was designated for Conner and Randy. But with two little ones in tow, I no longer had the time or energy to figure out how to compensate for sounds I could not hear. Those beeps, buzzers, and rings were now going undetected, even as some posed a safety concern. Nuggets were burned in the oven, food was left overnight in the microwave, and clothes were left in the washing machine to dry.

One day, without thinking, I decided to go to the fast-food drive-through with my boys. I shouldn't have done it and I knew it. I don't know why I couldn't accept that it simply wouldn't be possible. I should have remembered that the intercom sounds like a cheap walkie-talkie. But I decided to try in order to avoid carting two small children into the restaurant. I was a tired mom.

The attendant at the intercom couldn't get her message to me after multiple attempts. When I drove to the window, she took my money and tossed the bags of food into my vehicle. We received wrong orders due to my mishearing. I was upset at my sons for being noisy little kids and they were upset with me for being upset! From that day forward, we went inside for fast food. Sharply observant of the workers' ordering procedures, I read lips and ordered meals with pretty good success.

Most hearing-impaired people are conditioned to be keenly aware of their surroundings. I was no different for most of my life until I had children. Now a mom, I was intensely focused on the kids first, then on my surroundings. This came to a head one night in the parking lot of a mega-market near my house. It was a quick trip that started well.

I pushed my cart through the aisles, not thinking about hearing anything except my internal voice reminding me of what I needed. When everything was collected and paid for, I briskly pushed my cart through the automatic doors leading out to the parking lot. My to-do list was almost complete. Last on the list was picking up my boys and going home. They would be hungry when I picked them up. Approaching my car, I pulled out my keys.

Then I felt something rushing toward me. Perhaps it was my sixth sense telling me that something was going on. But I was in a hurry so I focused on getting home, ignoring the negative energy around me. A man grabbed my shirt, bellowing, "Stop!" My shoulders rose up and I aggressively swung around to find a store attendant inches away from me. He was frantically directing me to do something, but I didn't know what. Pulling away from the man, I snarled at him to get away from me. Then I noticed his store badge.

Still a few inches from my face, he spoke to me once again. This time I could hear most of his voice and read his lips. Finally, I processed what had happened, his sentences fitting together like puzzle pieces. The security alarm had been ringing as I walked out of the store. The clerk had repeatedly requested to see my store receipts as I walked by. The alarm continued to ring as I marched through the parking lot, unaware of the alarm or the man walking after me—and he wanted to know why. I realized how suspicious it must have looked, but felt that he should never have grabbed at me from behind.

I handed him my receipt. Looking it over, he determined the alarm had not been set off by anything that I had stolen. Ironically, the cashier had failed to remove a security tag. Their own mistake had created this alarming situation. We went back into the store to remove the tag. When the transaction was complete, I told the man who had chased me down—in a voice that meant serious business— that if he ever touched me again I would kick him where the sun didn't shine. Furthermore, I explained, I had walked away while the alarm sounded because I did not hear it. I cannot hear it. And I will never hear it. But that didn't mean I was a thief. I went on to suggest that they add a set of flashing lights or other visual notification when the alarm goes off because the system as it stands is worthless to the deaf or hearing-impaired. There are many of us, even if you can't tell who we are.

When my feisty lecture was over, the man who had chased me down had a different expression: fear. Looking like a grandpa now instead of a security guard, with his thick glasses and three strands of hair, he stood silently for a few seconds. When he opened his mouth to speak, I was ready for anything. But he surprised me. He said, in the kindest, tender, most sincerely charming voice, "You are sooooooooooo beautiful." Then he looked me in the eye, waiting for a reaction.

I laughed out loud. Then shook my head as we parted ways. Good save, Grandpa! I thought as I was heading back to my vehicle. I was glad that I hadn't pitched a long, nasty fit, because I needed to get home and cook dinner for my boys.

As Little Bit grew older, he became aware of his surroundings, interacting with his big brother and enjoying any kind of stimulation. Innocently, he called out to "Nonner', not yet able to say Conner's name correctly. I couldn't tell the difference and Conner didn't seem to mind, so the name Nonner was used and accepted by family for several years. Soon enough, Little Bit moved out of the baby bouncer and into Nonner's old baby swing. This swing had six speed settings. Nonner had always preferred the speed set on number three, so I decided to use the same setting for Little Bit. After placing Little Bit in the swing, I would do a variety of mom stuff around the house or take an occasional nap. Meanwhile, Nonner played in the same room with his brother. Now three years old, Nonner was my right-hand man, watching over the baby for me as I shuffled around the house. Little Bit found the view amusing, oftentimes giggling himself to sleep.

On a cool fall Saturday afternoon as I was folding clothes, Nonner walked in to tell me someone was at the door. "How do you know?" I asked, and he responded matter of factly: "Cause someone is knocking, Momma." Good enough for me. He went back to drawing in the back room while I walked to the kitchen and opened the door to see one of my colleagues. After I let her in, she looked around the kitchen, puzzled. "What is that noise?" she asked.

I listened carefully, but heard nothing. No music, no TV, nothing. I liked to keep the house quiet when it was time for the baby to nap. At least, to my ears, it was quiet.

"I don't hear anything—what does it sound like?" I asked.

"It's a really fast clicking noise, like someone tapping on the table with a key," she said.

I walked around the kitchen, looking in the sink, the refrigerator, and the pantry as she followed me, though I had no idea what I might be looking for. I wasn't sure whether this sound had occurred before, without me knowing it, or if it was some new sound.

"It's coming from another room—back there." She motioned to the back of the house. A pang of worry suddenly hit my stomach— the sound she heard was coming from the baby's room. I turned and walked toward the back room as my colleague trailed me close behind.

"That's where it's coming from!" she said. As we turned the corner and entered the room, there sat Little Bit, his tiny body wrapped in a snuggly suit and strapped to his swing that was rocking back and forth so rapidly it was dizzying to look at. And propped upright on tray of the fast rocking swing was an 8"x10" framed photo of Nonner, strategically placed in front of Little Bit so that it was his only view. My friend looked horrified, as if a ghost was aggressively yanking the swing back and forth.

I hurried over and turned the swing off, scooped up Little Bit, and held his groggy little body in my arms. I noticed the speed setting was on six, the fastest possible speed. This wasn't the speed I had it set on a few hours earlier. My colleague backed away slowly, obviously startled, and maybe a little bit spooked. "What happened to your swing? Did it malfunction?" she asked.

From down on the floor where he'd been drawing with his markers, Nonner spoke up, proudly taking responsibility. "I did it. I turned it all the way. He likes it."

Hearing Nonner's voice, Little Bit awoke, giggling and grinning as he lifted his head from my shoulder to peer at me and then at his brother.

"See?" Nonner exclaimed. "He likes it."

★   ★   ★

Little Bit proved to be a tough little lad, as I later learned one night. Something woke me up but I didn't know what. Looking around my bedroom in the dark, I could feel a negative energy permeating the house. As I continued the process of waking up from a deep sleep, I saw a red light out of the corner of my eye. It was the baby monitor. I had been keeping the volume on ten after my experience during Nonner's baby years, setting it on the pillow next to my ear each night. But this night, the monitor had fallen between two pillows. There was no way to determine how long Little Bit had been crying and why.

Though I could hear nothing coming from the monitor, red lights blared like muted police sirens. Little Bit was crying—I needed to go to him. My heart was beating fast as I ran through the house to his room. I found him crying in his crib and checked him from head to toe. His little body was hot and sweaty from crying, but he quieted down as I held him in my arms and kissed his head. All I could find was a wet diaper.

He was okay. But I wasn't. I felt like a dangerous influence on my own little boys. I had to come up with a better plan after discovering the baby monitor would no longer be of any help. It was useless. Was I useless too? I thought about the question all night.

Going against everything I had learned about caring for babies, I began putting Little Bit in bed with me at night. This arrangement would not foster his independence as a sleeper, but what mattered at that moment was having Little Bit safe and near his mommy. I would see to it that my baby boy would never again wake in the night and feel abandoned. This sleeping arrangement lasted several months until I finally decided to put Little Bit back into his crib just before his first birthday. Nonner generously offered to be the daddy and tell me when Little Bit was crying.

VIII. ROLLING WITH THE PUNCHES

Live and love, share and learn,

give and take, lose and earn,

cry and laugh, moan and groan.

Get it right, get it wrong, get it together,

and move right along ...

— S. L.

1999

*T*here is something magical about communicating with your offspring. The first year after a child's highly anticipated arrival, communication is predominantly nonverbal, mostly occurring through eye contact, expressiveness, various forms of physical contact, and the powerful human touch. As the child moves into sounds and listens to his parents' speech, he begins to mimic them, often babbling right along with their conversations. Parent and child converse excitedly as the child moves through his first word, phrase, or sentence. As parents, we savor every milestone that our child reaches.

The excitement and thrill of communication is doubled when our children begin communicating with one another. Video recorders are turned on and tape recorders are put to work. These precious moments can happen anywhere our children assemble together—at the dinner table, in the bedroom, on the sofa, in a car, in the sandbox—even in the bathtub.

When Little Bit first began interacting verbally with Nonner, one word in particular sent Little Bit into a giggle fit—"punkin." Each time Nonner said the word "punkin," Little Bit would repeat it in his own unique way, saying "bucket." Then Nonner would laugh and say "noooo, punkin," which of course sent Little Bit into hysterics. Soon they were both playing along just for the fun of it, with Little Bit saying "bucket" and Nonner replying "noooo, punkin." They replayed this exchange over and over each day. No other word had the same effect on either of them.

I tested my limits in order to make as many memories as we could. We sang songs, went to museums and parks, played baseball and other sports. With each activity, I learned more about my capabilities—and my growing disability.

My abilities were numerous—but limited, because of my one disability. In everything I did, there were constant struggles and upsetting new limitations imposed on me. Struggling was not a new event; but there were many new variants requiring different compensation techniques. It was a desperate fight to survive in a world that I had spent decades trying to figure out, but true grit moved me forward, even when the road led to the same old heartache.

Since the day I first heard it, music had lifted me from countless heartaches. Years later, after my sons were born, I cherished our sing-alongs. The stacks of songs I had collected over the years as a primary level teacher was a gift the three of us enjoyed as long as we could. In time I no longer could hear the words or music clearly but I was still able to remember how it sounded, and it was wonderful a feeling it was to sing with my boys. I couldn't tell whether they were actually learning the words or babbling nonsensically but it was joyous anyway. I would not stop making memories until there was nothing left to reach for.

I often cooked and baked with my boys, which was one of our most treasured activities to do together. However, my ability to communicate with my sons while we cooked began to deteriorate. I couldn't hear their voices amid the clanging of pots and pans—nor could I read their lips if I was busy with a mixer or a food processor. When Nonner was about five years old, I decided it was too dangerous to cook with my little guys because I couldn't keep a proper eye on four little hands reaching for the oven, or two little tongues licking the counter.

Next I began showing the boys how to make crafts. Once again, I started out confidently, always having enjoyed arts and crafts activities. We reveled at making gorgeous messes with glittery, gluey, gooey things, and even produced a great Christmas wreath or two when Nonner was five years old and Little Bit was two years old.

But soon enough, my abilities narrowed because I couldn't have a reciprocal conversation with my boys while keeping an eye on what they were doing. Reading the lips of not one but two little boys required my complete attention, preventing me from closely watching the other. X-Acto knives, glue, permanent markers, needles, scissors, and staplers in the hands of little children are not to be taken lightly, and eventually I had to close the craft box for good.

However, there were still other options for "mommy moments," such as museums, zoos, and sports. The first visits to a new museum were the best! At the largest natural history museum in Houston, Nonner and Little Bit were very impressed with the dinosaur skeletons. They spent the entire day smiling, or dropping their mouths open in awe. That first time at the museum, the three of us were together in spirit, sharing our joy. I was floating on a cloud of happiness because we were connected. In all the excitement, I didn't notice how noisy the museum building actually was.

A few months later on our second visit, I did notice. This time, my boys had much more to say than "ooh" and "ahh," chattering excitedly as I ushered them around in silence. The whole experience was supposed to be a shared one between my boys and myself but now it looked like it would be a brother-to-brother experience. I took the boys on a few more museum trips, accepting that I would be left out.

It wasn't all about me, anyway, so I tolerated those long, boring trips to the museum. The boys spoke to me often, happy and curious, but rarely could I hear them. I hoped my boys would remember my commitment to exposing them to the arts and sciences—with or without my conversation. That was the best I had to offer and so I did.

As frustrating as these experiences could be, there were moments of wonder for me as well. One day at the museum, I recognized something that had gone completely unnoticed until then. I watched the two brothers as they looked at each other, then giggled. There was more occurring between them than I thought. This went beyond two kids laughing about their favorite words— punkin and bucket. Conner and Randy were exchanging words I could not hear, but I could see them communicating. Only a few words a time—but yes, they were exchanging words with one another. Though I couldn't join in, the sight of my two sons verbally interacting was fascinating.

Limitations on what I could hear had been restricting my conversations for many years, but there was something new developing. As my hearing was deteriorating, so too was my speech. Stringing words together into a complete thought was now an effort, one that slowed down the whole communication process. Now I was not only slow to understand the meaning of conversations I could hear, I strained to remember words, include prepositions, and pronounce words correctly. All of this was too slow for a fast-paced conversation, especially with kids.

While they learned about rocks, I watched my two little boys interacting as brothers. It was happening right in front of my eyes in the midst of this hustling, bustling museum. I longed to participate in the moment but felt it was best if I didn't slow them down.

That special day at the museum, when little brother had his first conversation with big brother, was theirs to experience organically, without interruptions, so I just let it be.

Watching their developmental milestone unfold in the museum, it seemed that I had no more options for gaining an active, engaged place in my sons' world. I was being steadily shut out—and I had to stop it before I was completely disconnected from them, if there was even a way. Briefly, I thought about giving up. But with His perfect timing, the Lord placed two little warm sticky hands in mine. My two precious little men had each taken my hand in theirs—and it was settled. Onward I would march. I can, I will, and I must. That night, as I lay in bed in the dark, a question ran circles in my head. What would happen if I did give up?

This was a question that I had explored before. The next morning, as I sat in my favorite chair by the window, watching sunrays peeking through the treetops, just like that—I knew the truth. Giving up meant ceasing my fight to be a part of the world my sons lived in, the world I lived in. And even though I didn't have my own place there, that was where I was. It's where I wanted to be because it was what I want to be—the mother of two precious little boys. Giving up would mean losing the gift of being in the lives of my children, which was more important to me than anything else I could think of. It was a place worth fighting for.

I finally "got it." We would continue to move forward, not backward. We fought hard to understand one another wherever we were—in the car, at the store, at the museum, in restaurants, everywhere. Their young voices were beautiful and slight, their speech immature and developing. As my sons began to realize their mom was a little bit different than other people, they automatically repeated things or tapped my shoulder as a signal to read their lips.

★   ★   ★

Professionally, I had completed several postgraduate training hours to become a reading specialist. The courses had taken place in a small classroom with fewer than twenty students. This seemed to be customized for me, and I was successful in it. Excited and motivated, I enrolled in a formal grad school program, taking on a year of coursework. I was hungry for more personal and professional growth!

Instead, I stumbled into familiar frustrations from my undergraduate days. The classes were different but the challenges were the same. This time around, the academic material was twice as difficult; study groups were twice as demanding, and group presentations were impossible for someone who was always two steps behind.

I dropped out after a year, knowing that my grades were not indicative of the best I had to offer. Untapped potential is a tragedy. My hearing aids simply could not pick up an instructor's voice in a large auditorium. This had not changed since college. But the reading specialist certification was mine to keep forever. It was something that I had successfully accomplished on my own. For the next four years, I worked with first-graders who were struggling to learn how to read. Unbeknown to me at the time, this would be a stepping-stone into the next segment of my life.

IX. THE HARDER I FALL, THE HIGHER I BOUNCE

Years ago, and epochs gone past
a thirtyish woman went home to unpack,
seeking help from her mom on the long road uphill,
who answered, as always, "Yes dear, I will."

— S. L.

1999

*I*n the middle of July I awoke from a bad dream that I was a single mother. Only it wasn't a bad dream. I was a single mother. Going deaf was no longer the challenge I sought to overcome.

Wasting many nights, I lay in bed trying to understand the "why." On a full moon, I watched the clouds moving past my window. Simply and suddenly, I decided to stop worrying and start praying. Faith would be my weapon, releasing me from fear of the unknown. From my pillow, I gave my worries to God and, instead of "why" I asked "what next?" The next morning, I picked myself up, dusted off the seat of my pants, and marched right into my future. Ready to leave the past where it belongs—in the past—I turned a corner and started over with my two little boys. We were like rolling stones, shedding our moss along a bumpy road. Leaving my job to start over, I relocated across town to live with my mother for a short while. My sons were commissioned to live with their father until I could get back on my feet. It was a hard decision but the correct one. Though it was only a short-lived phase of transition, it was not my proudest moment.

During this process, my mother was crucial in supporting me in my new role as single mom, one who took on the task of hearing for me. We became very close. On the weekends, the four of us bonded in a way that had not been possible before I moved in. In awe, I watched interactions and growing relationships between Grandma and her grandsons, studying their facial expressions, voice inflection, and hand gestures. Their powerful interactions led to an intimate relationship of the very nature I had been seeking, but was always just out of reach.

I hadn't come to grips with truth of my life—that I was aggressively going deaf. But now it was obvious. There was vast difference between my interactions and Grandma's. She was giving the boys what they needed—a real connection. Her chats with Little Bit were loving and sweet, easily switching into high gear for lively conversations with Nonner, who had quite a bit to say due to his big brother status.

During this transition, I spent hours exploring the local school districts, hunting for an open teaching position. I was prepared to start completely over. Professionally speaking, I had all the credentials and capabilities to teach any subject at any grade level between one and eight, with a special certification as a reading specialist. Realistically speaking, however, I did not have the ability to teach a full classroom load of students in any subject, at any grade level. But I had to figure this out—I can, I will, I must. The limitations were not going to bring me down. I was thankful for having the chance to start over and determined to find my place in the world, praying that I would sooner than later.

The boys were growing older, and taking a greater role in helping bridge the gap between what I need to hear and what I couldn't. One could argue that my sons were forced to grow up a little faster than other kids their age, even as I tried to shield them from more pressures than they could handle at such a young age. They were my ears when I couldn't hear, telling me when an ambulance was approaching on the road, if a train was crossing nearby, or when the ice cream man was coming. They answered the phone for me, alerted me when the doorbell rang, warned each other of possible danger, and tattled on each other just like normal brothers. Without them, I could not have made it on my own—such a sad admission of the state of my affairs at the time.

I needed them greatly. But as their mother, they needed me as well, for clean clothes, hot dinners, and warm hugs. Our commitment to each other was a shared responsibility, like it or not. Both did seem to like it though, and were proud of their ability to notify me of something I didn't hear.

After four weeks of searching, I finally landed a teaching position in a new school district across town. Several months later, my sons and I were together again for our new beginning. We moved into a new home, a new neighborhood, a new school district, with new friends about to be made, and new memories waiting in the wings. Our new life together had started strong and the pendulum was swinging in our favor. I was savoring every moment.

The new job looked and felt like the perfect fit. I was lucky to have even come across the position, and even luckier to have been called in for an interview. The meeting, which was conducted by a few of the kindergarten teachers along with an interview committee, was very productive. One at a time, each committee member went through a list of pertinent questions, which I first thought about carefully, then answered quickly, professionally, and truthfully. I felt there was a positive chemistry between us, a very smooth rapport. The more the interview committee learned about me, the clearer it became that we were all on the same page in terms of educational philosophy, practical strategies, and resource allocation. I was sure that this was something I could do, and do very well, because I would be working with a group of four to six children in a private room, sitting at a small round table, making it quite possible to keep their voices within earshot and exceptionally easy to lip read for added support.

After a stimulating discussion on what I could offer, I shifted the conversation to what I could NOT offer. Humbly, I disclosed my inability to work in a classroom setting, either as an instructor or with small groups embedded within a full classroom setting. I explained that the noise level was a hurdle that I physically could not overcome. My final statement to them before the interview ended was one I hoped would remain in their minds about me after I left. I looked at the group earnestly and said, "I don't let what I can't do interfere with what I can do—and I can do this."

Remarkably, I started the job one week later. My new job as a kindergarten ELL small-group instructor promised to be both fascinating and challenging. Fascinating in the respect that I had never before worked with ELL students (students learning to speak English) or kindergarten students before; challenging because their little voices would barely be audible. Searching for the voice of a five-year-old would be the equivalent of looking for a needle in a haystack. There was only one action plan possible—I had to focus completely on lip reading during instruction.

The most intriguing aspect of my new position was the connection I already had with my students before I ever met them. The challenges each little English language learner faced every single day was staggering: five years old, many of them away from home for the first time, many in a new state or country, all spending seven hours a day understanding very little, or no language at all. They were confused, scared, lonely, tired, and withdrawn, and they spent every minute of every day trying to make sense of the world around them.

That was their world. It reminded me very much of mine. We had so much in common— above all, the need to be understood. And because I understood their world I also understood their special needs—among them, patience, eye contact, clear and concise articulation, extra wait time for a response, repetition when needed, and keen observation to determine moments of confusion or erroneous understandings. I was absolutely certain that the lessons and experiences from my lifelong effort to understand my world with a limited amount of information had provided me with the unique expertise needed to educate these very young children. Without having met them, I already knew that I loved them.

I understood and loved them in the way I wished that I had been in first grade. These were the things I could offer my new students, team, and principal. My hearing had been a monstrous negative for so long, and still was, but it was an amazing grace in my work with kindergarten English language learners.

My new team of colleagues proved to be just as revitalizing as my new career path. How lucky I felt to have the support of these amazing educators, who seemed assured that together we would meet our students' needs. We would simply work it out, regardless of my physical limitations. For now, they were confident in my abilities and believed in me.

The morning of my very first day at my new campus, the rollercoaster ride of life's ups, downs, and curves was in effect. Walking the halls, I admired the sheer enormity of the building, which housed nearly one thousand schoolchildren. I had never seen so many kids under one roof. Despite its size, the traffic in the hallways was quite organized and calm. But there was one little student standing off by himself, leaning against the wall, quiet and composed. I watched him curiously, noting that he was neither coming nor going, so I decided to investigate. The young man's big brown eyes studied me as I approached him with a smile and greeted him with a kind hello.

"Are you all right, son?" I asked, trying not to sound authoritative. He nodded without speaking. That was a yes, I thought, so all was well.

"Okay, great! Then move along and head down to your class," I said.

He responded but I was not able to decipher his meaning in the noisy hall. A thousand kids—it seemed like it was a thousand times harder to hear. But it was important to connect, so I asked him to repeat himself, which he did with a gentle, patient face. As he spoke, I moved closer to his face, watching his lips, and listened closely.

Nothing. I heard nothing! "Please, sweetheart, say it one more time for me." Intensely fixated on his lips, I struggled to hear what he was saying. This young man's mouth was moving, but nothing was coming out. It was frustrating because he needed some kind of help and I wanted to be there for him. Unfortunately, it was useless. I was completely deaf to the pitch of his voice and I had no way of reading his lips effectively because there was no context to his words. We looked at each other, without speaking, for several moments. Then I did the only thing I could think to do: I reached my hand out to his, my way of communicating care and concern for him without hearing or saying a word.

He understood—and responded by taking my hand. I escorted him to the school office, hoping that someone would help. What it was that he had been trying to tell me? Had he left his breakfast money at home? Was he in trouble for not having his homework?

At the office, I softly tapped on the secretary's window. She poked her head out and spoke to the young man. Turning back to me, she assured me that everything was fine and she would take care of the situation. With that, it was time for me to get going. I needed to make my own morning preparations for the day but I planned to return later to follow up on the little boy I had found standing in the hall.

By the end of the day, the mystery was solved. The nice-looking second-grade student, I finally learned, was a new student and he had forgotten where to go. What a surprise it was to discover that just like me, it was his first day! His parents had registered him the day before and dropped him off first thing that morning. After breakfast, he wandered around briefly and had simply lost his way. Like I had done in grade school, he had stopped in the hallway, hoping a teacher would understand his problem and come to his aid. But unfortunately for him, I was the person who stopped to help that day. He didn't get the verbal support he'd hoped for because I was completely deaf to his voice.

I talked this over with one of my colleagues, thinking I would feel better, but I didn't. It bothered me immensely. The only answer we came up with was for me to ask for help when I needed it, exactly as I had done. My colleagues felt this was a minor inconvenience because they had no idea of just how little I could hear. Many times after that day, I thought about the little boy who had lost his way, hoping he had found security and confidence. I wondered if I was becoming useless. While self-doubt tiptoed around me, I clung to the hope that I was here for a reason, not as a burden.

Soon after I started my new job, the kindergarten team leader and I came up with a plan that met everyone's needs. They would allow me to pull students from their classrooms so I could work with the kids in my own space, an empty room without noisy distractions. All I needed was a table, five chairs, books, crayons, paper, and pencils. My colleagues didn't always understand my ways but they accepted me as part of their team.

Though I did my best to offer my colleagues the same acceptance that they had bestowed upon me, I did not socialize with any of them at all—not after school, during school, or on the weekends. Going out with a group of women in a public setting would be going up a creek with no paddle. As nicely as I could, I declined their invitations to lunch, dinner, or happy hour and I stayed away from the teacher's break room. We worked well together and respected one another professionally, but outside of that, I didn't feel comfortable.

I also avoided the campus-wide social functions such as the Christmas party and the End of Year party. Because I couldn't hear at the social events, I couldn't socialize either. I dreaded having to don the "fake face" out in public when I was stuck in a noisy situation that I couldn't function in. By then it was undeniable—I had come to the point of avoiding social situations, and people in general, because someone might speak to me. I often wondered if they would be disappointed in who I really was and the amount of work it took to have a relationship with me.

But time would offer opportunities to develop our professional relationships. Mutual trust within the team was being built through collaboration, which gave me courage to share other issues as they came up. I was stepping into uncomfortable territory by exposing my growing list of limitations to a group—something I had never done before. Surprisingly, it felt good to talk frankly about the changes taking place in my life, both the good and the bad. All that was required of this never-ending series of problems was the will to solve them, and then move on. Had I not shared some of the most critical issues I faced, and received supportive, sound advice, the consequences would have been much more problematic.

I drew on these solid relationships as I battled the steady stream of complications caused by my inability to hear what I needed to hear, such as a phone call from a concerned parent early one Friday morning. I passed through the front office area as the phone was ringing—this I knew because it was lighting up like a passing fire truck. Looking around, I realized there was no one in the office to pick up the phone! I wanted to sneak away, but for some particular reason, I decided that the call must be taken. At the very least, I needed to try.

"Hello?" I asked nervously.

"*Wa wa wawa wa wawawa wa.*"

"Excuse me, could you repeat that?" I asked. My heart was racing.

"*Wa wa wawa wa wawawa wa.*"

And with that, I panicked. The thin ice I was standing on gave way as I looked around for a lifeline. How I wished someone would pass through the office. I saw the intercom just a few inches from the phone. It would quickly summon a teacher, but I had never learned to use it. It was another device I had stayed away from because I couldn't hear much of anything announced over the intercom anyway.

I continued to struggle through the panic, thinking as quickly as I could of a way to communicate with this person on the phone. If I could just understand the words! Oh, how I wished I could help this person! I put down the phone and ran from office to office in search of someone to help. When I found another staff member, she rushed over and picked up the phone. Effortlessly, she talked the caller through the issue and hung up.

But it wasn't over. This parent wasn't happy about the treatment she had received. Who could blame her? The issue, as I was told later, was her daughter's report card. She wanted to meet with her child's teacher to discuss her concerns.

After taking this problem to my colleagues, they offered to take phone calls from parents for me in the future. All I had to do was ask. Instead I just avoided any and all types of phones whether they were ringing or not. Those who knew me understood why I did this. Those who did not know me personally concluded that I was a slacker for not picking up a ringing telephone. At the end of the day, it didn't matter what they perceived because I knew that I was doing what I had to.

At a "Meet the Teacher Night" a few years later, I struck up a conversation with a woman who went on to tell me of a very unpleasant experience she'd had with someone in the front office. She talked about how frustrated she was that the person she had spoken to could not "get it." After identifying myself as being the person who she had spoken to, I apologized sincerely but didn't explain the reason why we couldn't communicate. Her response to my apology was her own humble admission that she had come to believe the person she had spoken with was retarded. Though her comment was not meant maliciously, it was cutting. It did not surprise me, however, because I had already heard the same comment several decades before.

Critical issues came up more than once that year. On a very normal day, as I was passing through the school cafeteria, a first-grade student walked up to me with a question. I knew this was the very LAST place I should attempt to hear a child but I could not ignore him. Since the cafeteria was such a noisy setting, I zeroed in on his face and read his lips. It was a simple request: he asked if he could have some ketchup. I scanned the cafeteria serving line for the ketchup dispenser or small ketchup packets and saw that the lunch offering that day was pizza. No hamburgers, no nuggets, no corndogs. So I leaned down close to the first-grade student and told him, "We don't have any."

He looked at me with a blank stare, then asked me the same question. "Can I have some ketchup?" This time I made it simple and just said no. Before I could walk away, this little fella tugged my shirt and asked one more time—"*Please*, can I have some ketchup?" And once again, I told him, "No, we don't have any today." The student then went back to his place at the lunch table as I continued on my way.

Later on that day, my colleagues spoke of a student who had an "accident" during lunch. When asked why he didn't go to the restroom, the student explained that he had tried—but when he asked, the teacher had told him no, that "we don't have any today." I felt tremendous guilt about the little boy, though it was just a terrible misunderstanding. It was time to polish my lip-reading skills to prevent this type of "accident" from repeating itself. Starting right there and then, I focused 100% of my attention on any individual I was addressing, or who was addressing me. Additionally, I sought clarification when in doubt. I wanted to be of help, of value, and to live a life of purpose. How tired I was of always needing someone, even for the simple things like answering a phone or helping a child!

Being completely autonomous and independent was always so important to me, but had I been truthful with myself, perhaps I would have conceded long before that I had lost much of both abilities. After this incident I knew it was time to accept whatever was left and move forward with it.

But much to my chagrin, these types of dilemmas continued to develop. I worked through them all until one shattering event kicked me square in the gut, confronting me with the worst mistake I had ever made.

On a very normal day when my schedule was running smoothly, I had been pulling small groups into my teaching area for lessons. Somewhere in the two o'clock hour, all three of my students simultaneously looked up at me without speaking, then looked over at the door. It struck me as odd and I could not make meaning of it. I continued on with my lesson, directing them to remain focused so we could finish our lesson. They did. Then I sent them back to their classrooms.

After school, my colleagues' spoke about how well their students had behaved during the day's fire drill as I stood by silently. Was I reading their lips correctly? A fire drill ... today ... kids behaving ... then it hit me. My students had been staring at the doorway because they had heard the alarm going off but didn't know how to tell me.

I don't know how I made it to the restroom on my wobbling legs. I rushed into the stall, locking the door behind me, then leaned on the back of the door for support and hung my head in shame. Heavy tears fell to the floor as I prayed for guidance. Please, God, help me. Is this the end? What. Do. I. Do. Now?

As the tears dried, fear fell from my back. Peace overcame me and I realized that the way out of this incredible setback was up to me. Hope was not a strategy, only a source of strength. I had to put together a plan before the next fire drill or I would quit my job. Just as I had a plan to care for my sons, I needed a plan to care for my students, because they were mine too. It was time to once again talk to my team.

With a much dignity as I could muster, I put my heart and soul out there for them to see as I explained what had happened and opened the discussion to possible solutions. They were in disbelief—I think it was hard for them to understand that a person could truly not hear a fire alarm because the sound was so intense, almost painful. They gave me the benefit of the doubt, rationalizing that the kids may have been quite rowdy or we might have been singing a song when the alarm sounded. We worked our way through it and a plan was put into action. My students would be taught to line up immediately when the alarm sounded, just as they did in their homeroom classes, without waiting for me to react. As an added precaution, the closest colleague would pop her head into my room, giving me a heads up. In hindsight I realized that the concerned, puzzled looks from my students that day were the same looks from the swimmers in college when the phone was ringing at the pool. I was thankful that I would not have to encounter that look again.

We had placed a band-aid on the problem for the time being, but the long-term implications were still developing. The following afternoon after work, I sat down in the office of my audiologist, Tony, ready to find a fix for this discouraging state of affairs. I had convinced myself that my hearing aids were failing, not my ears.

X. TEAMWORK

Am I humble enough to acknowledge
that I'm really not all that tough?
Can I honestly admit to myself
that my best may not be enough?

—*S.L.*

2001

I'm sorry, that's the best it's going to get."

Those words didn't sound right. "What?" I asked, though I knew exactly what my audiologist had said. Tony looked me in the eye with honesty and sincerity. Why was he looking and sounding so serious? I tried not to understand, but there it was on a graph, and he was spelling it out in plain English. I had profound hearing loss, most of which hearing aids could not help—and that was that. The best I could walk out with was louder, more intense white noise.

The phrase "This is the best it's going to get" meant nothing to me. It couldn't be the best because I was failing. So it had to get better than this because this challenge must be overcome. But Tony's words were real pieces of truth, clearly indicating that my career would end one day. Unless a miraculous new hearing aid was introduced, very soon I would be deaf. Without my hearing, I would be useless, and even more useless, I'd be without a job. That night I couldn't find a moment of sleep, spending hours trying to wrap my mind around the idea of losing my calling, a life I had dedicated to kids.

Returning to work the next day, I felt great honor and a fresh respect for my role in the lives of children for more than two decades. Much more than a profession, teaching was a gift. I had spent twenty years cultivating my ability to make use of this gift. I lived each moment as if it might be my last in education. Every day spent as a teacher was the best day of my life.

With the knowledge that it could end soon, I worked harder to do the things I did well even better. My mind stayed focused on the things I could do as I tried not to let what I couldn't do get in my way. The noise level at school functions rendered me incapable of interpersonal communication, so I looked for new ways to contribute something meaningful.

At "Meet the Teacher Night", we were told to talk with parents and answer their questions. But since the hall was massively congested with parents and students and the noise was earsplitting, I compensated by ushering the parents to classrooms nonstop for two hours. At PTO meetings, I would found a quiet place to talk with parents. At carnivals, dances, and award ceremonies, I was the photographer, taking hundreds of photos and sometimes adding them to the school yearbook. At "Family Literacy Night", I took charge of a game located on the stage, away from the thunderous noise.

Though I could hear very little, and oftentimes nothing, I always found a way to do my part. Mistakes were made and miscommunications were common, and some of my colleagues looked at me suspiciously when I performed different duties than what they thought I should be doing, but I didn't give up. Exhaustion and migraines were the side effects, but I noticed that all the educators suffered during these highly stressful, physically exhausting activities.

I appreciated everyone's willingness to work with me as I endlessly tried to find a place where I could be useful. Because of the collaboration between my team, administrators, colleagues, and friends, the role I played, though different than the others, had purpose and value, giving me purpose and value as an educator. There were a few situations when acquaintances or colleagues knew there was something different about me—though no one ever said a word.

Such was the case when I disappeared during the annual "Beginning of Year Convocation", where all employees in the district met in a very large auditorium. While my colleagues occasionally wondered about my whereabouts, I was sneaking up to the front of the auditorium so I could hear the speaker better and read lips—at least for a little while. Some called it my "disappearing act." To me, it was no act—this was who I was and what I needed. And I accepted it. Outwardly, however, I didn't want to admit that I was this needy. Nor did I want to be thought of handicapped—and I certainly did not want to be seen as disabled. Denial is a cloak that I wore to conceal my impairment from others, though I couldn't hide it from myself.

After several years of "disappearing," moving to the front no longer helped. So I stayed with my group for what seemed to be days instead of a few hours. I felt trapped in my padded, comfortable chair, miles away from the stage, oblivious to the jokes that made my colleagues laugh out loud, and the inspirational moments that brought tears rolling down their cheeks. How I wished I could be a part. These moments were a déjà vu—I thought that I had conquered them for good many years before.

There were other situations when I missed meetings, left faucets running, teakettles whistling, my car motor running— events that continued to repeat themselves with much more frequency. My many caring colleagues took time to call my attention to urgent situations needing to be resolved. One very kind person even generously offered to jump-start my vehicle after I had left the headlights on! I'd never heard the bell indicating the lights were on. We laughed about those things outwardly, but after happening time after time, we all knew these were significant problems needing to be dealt with. I have never expected other people to be responsible for my troubles, and my ability to face them and solve them represented the last little bit of fight I had left. I might not be able to do the same things as everyone else, but I had to believe could still take care of myself and solve many of my own problems, even if I really couldn't. Asking for help was not easy for me to do, nor was it pleasing to my pride, so I dodged doing so whenever possible, fiercely holding on to my dignity.

My colleagues and I worked together for several years to deliver the best academic instruction we had to offer our students while working through the obstacles that came our way. The trust and respect between us soared, but an invisible wall was slowly forming. This wall was created by my increasingly introverted behavior as my hearing deteriorated. As badly as I had always wanted to be a hearing person and have a place in their world, I never could have a place, never would have a place—because although I could hear, I could *not* hear. It made no sense years ago and it made no sense now.

We always tried to understand each other as far as it could go, continuing to work in harmony for years, across separate worlds. Though I dreamed all my life of somehow finding my way into their world, I was resigned to accept that I would never make it there. Later on my colleagues told me that they noticed a change taking place in me—I was shifting from a bubbly, positive, energetic prankster to a quiet, serious recluse.

To compensate for not contributing to the team as much as I wanted to, I stayed up late at nights writing educational grants for our students as well as songs and poems for my lessons. It was my way of contributing because I could not contribute to the team in the traditional way—going into their classrooms, attending social gatherings, engaging them in hallway chats, eating lunch with the team, and having telephone conversations. Over a period of several years, money was awarded to grants I had written, allowing me to offer students innovative instructional activities that I hoped would have a positive impact on their learning. But most of all, the grants gave me value. I was, at least for the time being, outrunning failure. It didn't matter that I could still see, smell, and taste failure just behind me—right now I was winning.

My close-knit group of colleagues had no idea that I was so close to disaster, but they did know that I was fighting the fight of my life. They were my heroes, going to bat for me time and time again. In one situation, a colleague drew a line in the sand when another person became extremely irate that I wasn't performing the same duties as her. "Are you deaf or something?" the teacher screamed at me when I didn't take orders from her. After hearing of this, my colleague demanded ethical, professional behavior from the woman in question.

In another instance, my position was in danger of being dissolved to create a position for a classroom teacher. My colleagues stepped up for me, offering positive feedback about my instructional performance to our supervisors and team leaders. It was a show of loyalty that probably saved my job. Many times over, they fought for me—and fought for my needs. And though the things I needed were far more complex than normal, I never felt like I was being singled out as a "special needs" employee. I would continue the fight to make it in their world, the hearing world, with a little help from my friends. They were my strength.

Only on a few instances was I outwardly weak, breaking down in front of them, though once was in the presence of my team leader and then later on with my principal. When I lost my composure and self-confidence, there were no pity parties given me. Because they are outstanding educators, my team leader and my principal knew that the kind of "help" I truly needed was to help me to help myself. Instead of "saving" me, they encouraged and motivated me to pick myself up, problem solve, and move forward. Their high expectations made me a better, stronger teacher, mom, and woman.

But it was a lonely journey and I completely broke away, isolating myself from the team while trying to remain productive. Whether I was productive or not in the eyes of others made no real difference at the end of the day. The only thing that mattered was to honor my calling and serve my purpose: to reach and teach the little ones.

★   ★   ★

In 2006 a nearly deaf woman made a difference by saving someone's life. That woman was me. One day I noticed a woman slumped over in her vehicle as I waited at a red light. Her car was coasting slowly out into a busy intersection. This was a 911 situation. I quickly looked at my phone, but there simply wasn't enough time to call 911. I assessed the situation again for an alternative, and I knew what had to be done.

Looking up and down the street, I put my truck into park, and then I ran out into the intersection after the woman's car. As I reached the passenger side of her vehicle, I realized that the door was locked. I beat on the window, trying to break it as the car drifted into the path of oncoming traffic. I pounded on the window, trying to shatter the glass with my fists, but never even made a scratch. Then I looked around as I ran alongside the moving car, pleading with the drivers passing by to stop and help.

The other drivers just looked at me and drove off as if it were nothing out of the ordinary for a woman to be chasing down a driverless car on a busy six-lane road. Finally, out of nowhere, a big bulky man ran up to the driver's side door, which, as it turned out, was unlocked. He opened the door, stopped the car, and looked for any obvious injuries on the unconscious woman. "Can you call 911?" he asked. "My phone is in my car!" Then he began to push the car out of the path of oncoming vehicles.

I pulled out my phone—and panicked. 'How in the world am I going to do this?' I thought as I dialed 911. Nervously, I put the phone up to my ear and squeezed it as tight as I could. Then I waited. When I heard a faint sound, I didn't bother trying to decipher it. After quickly stating where I was and explaining what had happened, I told the operator that I could not hear on a phone because I was hearing impaired. The operator's response was unintelligible. I apologized for not being able to respond and hung up.

Within three minutes, the ambulance had arrived. I stepped back as the paramedics took over, watching as they removed her from the car. They questioned the man who had stopped and although I could not capture their conversation, I believe he reported the details leading up to their arrival. By then it was time for me to get out of the way and let the paramedics tend to the woman, so I carefully crossed back over six lanes of traffic, where my truck was parked at the red light where I had jumped out of it half an hour earlier. It was still there exactly as I had left it.

For a long time, my life had been such a struggle to live a life of purpose. Making a difference in children's lives was my pathway to self-worth. So chasing down the woman slumped over in her car was an extension of my calling to reach out.

Later that month as I wondered about the woman's condition, I contacted a friend who was a law enforcement officer and learned that she had suffered a seizure at the red light, just as I had pulled up beside her. My friend seemed very interested in how the events had unfolded that day, even coming to my office at work and asking me to recall each detail from start to finish. What I didn't know is that once she left my office, she went to the police station and discovered several taped 911 phone calls that were, oddly, not about the woman in distress. People had called in to report a wild woman chasing a driverless car going down the wrong way on a busy street. Some were concerned, others were angry, and still others were horrified.

A few weeks later, to my complete surprise, the local Chamber of Commerce contacted me about being selected as an Outstanding Citizen of the City of Houston. At a time when I was deeply in doubt about my self-worth and physical capabilities, how ironic it was that I had been selected as an Outstanding Citizen for stopping to help to a woman in need at a red light. I wasn't exactly sure what this meant, but I was absolutely positive that I had done the right thing. I used the award as fuel for my spirit, food for my personal resolve. This was the best day of my life.

★ ★ ★

At home, my growing boys had reached an age where their interactions were no longer giggles and goof offs. Now they were tattling. Those little tattles escalated into arguments, and the arguments almost always set off fights. My sweet, happy little boys were now at war. The arguments consisted of screams and hollers, so I heard them quite well, although the clarity of their shrieking words provided precious little information. I never knew "whodunit" or what it was all about. I wished mightily that I could participate more as a mother during these situations so they could learn how to grow through conflict. When I moderated their heated debates about who did what and who said what, I wasn't actually in the know. Perhaps other moms wouldn't miss listening to the daily disputes between their offspring, but for a mother who had very little to listen to at all, tattles were treasures.

Movies and television jumped into the scene as soon as Little Bit could sit through a whole movie. Like all of our "first times," the first movie we saw together was amusing and satisfying. Nothing can quite compare to watching a child lose himself in a movie, whether he is squealing in delight, laughing hysterically, or latching on to his mother's arm in fright. Children don't just view a movie, they LIVE the movie—because their minds cannot distinguish the difference between reality and what they see happening on a big stadium-sized screen. They are the heroes saving the world, protecting its people, chasing the bad guys, and triumphing over evil.

But after the thrill of our first few movies together, I found the films woefully difficult to stay interested in. Using visual cues such as reading lips, facial expressions, and body language to make up for a lack of auditory cues was sufficient at best, and it left a lot to be desired during a fast-moving cartoon with oddball-looking characters. And because I was completely exhausted all the time, visual cues just didn't cut it during full-length movie cartoons. I was usually asleep half an hour after the opening credits.

Taking kids to the movies became frustrating for all us when they began speaking to me in the dark—which, of course, is what kids do—they talk during the movie. Each question or comment from my son went unanswered unless we walked clear out into the lobby where I could read lips, which we rarely did. This didn't sit well with either of them—so they stopped speaking to me at the movies. And that didn't sit well with me. I felt like I was on the horns of a dilemma—take my sons to the movies and fall asleep or don't take them to the movies ... and stay at home with two very disappointed little boys. Since this was not about me, I chose to take them to the movies, falling asleep almost every single time.

Each time it felt as if a robbery had taken place. Another opportunity to grow closer to my children stolen away. I also felt like I was lazy and unmotivated for not being able to stay awake during movies. In reality, I was teetering on the brink of total exhaustion almost all the time. I was in the middle of a physical, emotional, and spiritual storm, fighting for my place in the world every second of every day of my life ... fighting to hear, fighting to read lips, fighting to understand body language and facial expressions, fighting to be a good mother and fighting for my place in the world. All of these things had become so difficult.

Oddly, doctors and dentists became my new best friends. For several years, there was a steady stream of doctor visits—for loose teeth, chicken pox, ear infections, pink eye, swine flu, asthma, eczema, and school vaccinations. My sons stepped up to the plate during doctor visits when they became aware that I wasn't hearing things that I needed to hear. Without complaint, they took on the role of hearing for me, signaling to me in the waiting room when their names were called for their turn to see the doctor. As the nurses led us to a check-up room, they held on to my hand— something I needed more than they did—until they reached an age when it was simply uncool to hold your mother's hand. And when we sat in the examination room together, their voices were confined to the small space within the four walls, enabling us to share a few sweet minutes of small talk before the doctor arrived.

My boys were soon helping me hear the doctors themselves, repeating to me what the doctor said or correcting information that I might have heard incorrectly. In other words, they had to play "mom."

It didn't seem appropriate that a child be placed in that kind of a situation. I felt they were too young to take on adult responsibilities—especially MY responsibilities—because I was the momma and they were my children.

One night after a challenging day at the dentist, I decided to hit the hay early. I fell into bed, released a long, worn-out sigh, and before I realized it was happening, tears were rolling down my cheeks. I knew I was having a weak moment triggered by fatigue and frustration, and that it would pass through prayer and by walking through it one step at a time. So I closed my eyes and spoke to Jesus. A few words into my prayer, I just stopped. "Lord, are you listening?" I was losing my faith ... losing my hope ... losing sight of my future.

"Help, me, Jesus. Please. Save me from this big mountain I am falling down. I have been tumbling down for so long, Lord, waiting for you to pick me up. I am so tired of this world."

Silence.

"You put me here, Jesus, but I don't belong!"

Tears.

"Jesus, I am letting everyone I love down." All of my feelings, all my fears and trepidations poured out of my heart and into that prayer. I held my breath and closed my eyes tight, as if my words might make it to Jesus faster that way. Then I waited in silence, expecting to hear something back. After so many years of praying, I was almost out of faith. I waited several minutes, for some kind of recognizable intervention in the form of something ... somewhere ... somehow.

As I stared into the darkness, I received no message, or at least nothing recognizable. I had asked Him to step in and He hadn't. But someone else did, and maybe it was part of His plan.

XI. A REASON TO BELIEVE

There's a man in my life who shares
himself, his life, his cares.
100% loyal and true,
there's nothing he wouldn't do.
He's the man I call
when I'm about to fall ...

— S.L.

2002

I met a man who was great fun to be with. Ray rode a motorcycle, was adventurous and intelligent, with a wickedly dry sense of humor, keeping me on my toes. He became my hero the night my truck broke down on a country road. Two hours into a trip to Austin, Texas, my truck stalled out for no apparent reason in front of a small rural gas station that had already closed for the evening. I picked up my phone to call someone, something I rarely did except in emergencies. But I was surprised to discover that my phone was dead. That was not good.

Surveying the situation in front of the gas station, I spotted a pay phone in the dark. I had no other choice but to grab my credit card and walk over to the pay phone, which was just a few feet away from the gas station building. I picked up the receiver. It was dead! I had a second thought, though—perhaps I just hadn't heard the dial tone. So I decided to pick up the receiver once again, this time punching in my credit card number and waiting for any kind of response. There was a response this time, the distant voice of an operator— but I could not make out any words. I tried again, hoping for a better connection, without any luck. It was now 10:30 P.M. I went back to my truck to rethink the situation.

From the front seat of my truck, I looked in all directions. In the pitch black of a country road, this place appeared to be a one-horse town. I could see no other business anywhere in sight and no lights in either direction. Taking a deep breath, I sighed heavily, almost breaking into a laugh, not knowing what else to do.

I walked back to the payphone, picked up the receiver, and dialed 911. I had done this once before in an emergency, and perhaps I could do it again. Pressing the phone tightly to my ear as I could, I waited for any hint of a voice. There was nothing. I tried again. Still nothing. On the third time, I heard a crackling, far-away noise, possibly that of a garbled message. I told the operator that I was hearing impaired and stated my name. I explained where I was and said that I was unable to use a telephone. Then I gave the name and number of my friend in Austin. There was a distorted response, useless to my broken ears, so I apologized for not being able to hear and hung up. Then I waited in my truck for something to happen.

Fifteen minutes later, a state trooper pulled up. He told me they had contacted my friend in Austin and that he was on his way to help. The trooper stayed with me for almost an hour, until he was dispatched to another emergency call. Before he left, he told me to call 911 again if my friend didn't show up—if I told the operator who I was she would send someone out. I locked myself in the truck, looked at my watch (it was past midnight), and fell asleep.

Sometime after one A.M., I awakened to someone knocking on my window. It was Ray. He had driven out in the dark on his motorcycle to help me. We briefly laughed about the situation before hopping on the motorcycle and riding into the night. We came back the next day to see whether the truck would start so that we could get it to the garage. When it didn't, we knew the truck would have to be towed back to my home two hours away. The truck never came back to life, but a lasting friendship was born, and love was in bloom, whether we knew it or not.

Our relationship was a celebration—we had become a family. The focus was no longer survival. I carried myself as a strong, independent woman but with one more person to hear, I was continuously running around after him asking to repeat what he had said. He was equally frustrated with our inability to understand each other. This was all part of the learning curve of our relationship.

Initially I held my own, attending to the doctor appointments, teacher conferences, and shopping with my sons acting as my translator. Then, slowly, Ray began removing the weight of those things from my sons and taking them on himself. I knew this guy was a keeper, because he was always there for me, sometimes even before I knew I needed help. I recognized him as a person I could trust with my life and the life of my sons.

I went to Ray one evening humbly asking for his support in a few challenging situations I had not been able to overcome. Immediately showing care and concern, he asked me what I needed. "A good pair of ears?" I joked. This was, in fact, the reality—I needed Ray to hear for me. Willingly, patiently, and lovingly, he offered his ears in order to help me when I could not help myself.

Just after the milestone of moving in together, he had his first experience as a hearing man living with a hearing-impaired woman, and it almost cost him $399. It all began with a telephone call. Trying to impress my boyfriend with a small degree of independence, I answered the phone. The voice was loud but barely decipherable. I heard a scratchy-voiced fast talker, someone I didn't recognize. I wondered if this might be my worst nightmare—a telemarketer. They were incredibly smooth, sometimes even pretending to know me. "Telemarketer or not, all I need to do is say 'no thank you' and hang up," I told myself.

But before I could hang up, I heard something recognizable and was excited. It felt good to hear something on the phone! The salesperson asked if I liked taking cruises, and I replied yes. That was the only word other than "Hello" I uttered during the entire phone call. He said a few more things, then said goodbye, and hung up. After the phone call ended, I glanced over at my boyfriend. Everything seemed to be okay. It looked like I had saved face. Whew!

The next morning as I was preparing for school, my boyfriend came to me with a piece of paper in hand. We sat down together as he shared a concern. "Did you buy a four-day cruise for $399?" he asked. I laughed out loud. He was not laughing along and I realized it wasn't a silly joke. "Of course I didn't. What are you talking about?" I asked. Then I became nervous. I had no idea what was going on but something in my gut was telling me that whatever it was, it was entirely my fault. Ray went on to explain that our credit card account had been charged $399.

He investigated the charge, scrutinizing the origins of the company while I was at work. As soon as I walked in the door that afternoon, he announced the answer to the $399 question. In fact, I had purchased the cruise—over the telephone the day before. I denied it, of course. The man had asked only one question: "Do you like going on cruises?" It didn't seem possible that I had could have purchased a cruise just by saying yes. The next hour was spent on the phone conferencing with the credit card company and reporting the scam.

After that experience, we decided I should stop answering the telephone, with the exception of taking calls from a handful of people. There were a few whose voices I knew exceptionally well—so well that I could guess the parts of words that I could not hear. They were the lucky ones, I suppose—at least for the time being. Later on, the list would shrink to zero.

For the time being, I would enjoy the things I could still do, especially with my family. Together time was precious, yet seemingly growing scarce as the boys were growing older. As they matured, we grew apart in a natural progression of social development. But I still had dinnertime—an irreplaceable opportunity for mother/son moments. It was a tremendous joy to fully participate in reciprocal conversations. Seeing my family at close range at the dinner table allowed me to read lips quickly. I responded to them with much more ease than in any other situation other than a one-on-one, face-to-face dialogue. Such a treat! In the furthest corners of my consciousness, I worried that future opportunities to connect with them would decline, so I focused all of my energy and heart on dinnertime. We shared some laughs, as well as our daily highs and lows in what we aptly called the Hi-Low Game. It was not unusual for me to spontaneously exclaim, "This is the best day of my life!" during those dinnertime chats.

My heart joyously spoke of the "best day of my life" during many ordinary moments. Each shared experience between the four of us at the dinner table was—for me—a mammoth, priceless gift. The connection with my sons and my boyfriend was completely extraordinary to me, something I had never experienced in my life. For so many years each moment had been wholly about survival, but now I was able to capture a few moments of pure joy.

Away from the dinner table, a new kind of connection was born when I began riding a motorcycle. It was a connection to freedom. Going against my better judgment, I took a ride on the back of a motorcycle and was instantly hooked. The freedom of detaching myself from stress and riding with the wind was life changing. A few months later, with encouragement from friends and family, I learned how to drive my own motorcycle. Riding with the wind was a rare thing that I could do without the need to hear well. My motorcycle represented freedom—MY freedom. My first road trip to Colorado, a 2,000-mile round trip, was the best vacation of my life because I was completely free and I felt integrated with nature—riding through mountain, prairie, and open range environments. I did not ever want to stop riding, or end this feeling of freedom.

One day, after a long, cool ride in the national forest, the sun descended on a pleasant Valentine's Day, and a surprise awaited me at the kitchen table. As I lay in bed with my laptop propped open, my sons popped their head in the room, asking that I come into the kitchen, then scurried away. In the kitchen, I found my boyfriend and sons waiting for me, standing together in a semicircle. I was confused and scanned the room for clues. Helium-filled balloons lined the kitchen ceiling, forming a sort of word train. On each balloon was a letter handwritten in magic marker. As they watched in total silence, I scanned the letters on the balloons, sounding out each word as I decoded it:

W-I-L-L-Y-O-U-M-A-R-R-Y-M-E-?

Startled, I glanced over at my boyfriend, then at my boys who were smiling with eyes wide open. Magic was in the air and there was only one possible answer to the question. We all knew what was about to happen. Because I didn't have to hear in order to experience this moment, I melted into it. All that I wanted, all that I had, and all that I would ever need was surrounding me in a circle of warm, smiling faces. Through a smile and a tear, I turned to Ray and said yes while the boys cheered us on. My fiancé placed a ring on my finger, and an angel necklace on each son. This was the best day of my life.

Later that night, I briefly walked outside to let the moment settle in. Here I was, a woman going deaf and becoming dependent on those around her—and here, also, was a man capable of deep, durable love. I wondered if it was a miracle that we had found each other, a gift of amazing grace from Heaven. It didn't matter, I supposed, because that night I would go to sleep as a woman who was spoken for. Standing in the peaceful darkness of the nighttime outdoors, I closed my eyes, held my head up, and took in another long, deep, sighing breath.

When I opened my eyes, a familiar figure in the night sky was looking back at me—a full moon. Alongside the shining moon were a few scattered stars, reminding me of the dreams that had already come true, those that were in the process of coming true, and the dreams that were yet to be. That night, instead of confusion and worry, I felt happy, content, and relieved that I would not be facing the frightening future alone. I let go of a chunk of negative energy and doom I had been carrying around for decades, the grief that had been pushing me into a hole. With the help of my future husband, I had crawled out of the hole.

I thought about the prayer I had made years before as I cried in bed, begging for help in finding a way to survive in this world without the resources I needed. I remember being so frustrated and desperate that night that I had given up praying altogether, thinking there was no amazing grace after all. I was wrong. Praying had actually helped.

He did hear me. Maybe my future would not be filled with sadness. Maybe I had a place in this world. There were lots of maybes, and they were all good. I thanked God. On that day, I reclaimed my faith and hope.

XII. NEVERMIND

I don't know why it happened the way that it did.

You don't know, but I'll love you as long as you live.

I can't tell you the things that I want you to hear,

you can't hear what I say if you won't come near.

I didn't give you the love I needed to give,

you didn't give yourself a chance to forgive.

Faithfully I wait for a second chance,

with a hopeful heart and outstretched hands.

—*S.L.*

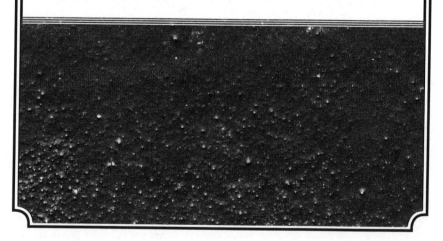

2006

On a hot October night, a blended family was officially born in our backyard. Our routine had already been established so making it official wasn't much of an interruption. There were, however, interruptions of a different kind. Two years into marriage, I woke up completely deaf for the first time in my life. It lasted about fifteen minutes, and during that short time, I could not even hear a door slam. Since it was only temporary, I decided it must have been a fluke. Avoidance is a coping mechanism that does not last very long.Then it happened again. And again. Episodes of temporary deafness intermittently reoccurred through the weeks and months. Avoiding the implications of these incidences, I kept them to myself. It was clearly a case of denial, when I should have been preparing for the worst. Denial is not an effective coping mechanism, and the stress associated with sudden deafness manifested itself in panic attacks. The attacks started as mild experiences but intensified as my hearing deteriorated.

★　★　★

As the episodes of deafness continued, the routines I had established began to unravel as my hearing deteriorated faster than I could reroute my plans in order to compensate. Uncomfortable situations and problematic mistakes occurred regularly, especially when my sons' teachers called, not knowing I was practically deaf.

I had taken their calls using speakerphone, hoping for the best, but finally I insisted that they teachers call my husband instead of me.

Once Ray took over, the complications disappeared. After each phone call, he explained the situation and we worked out a solution. Then the two of us would talk to our sons at dinner, with my husband conscientiously drawing me into the conversation so I could contribute. I accepted this reduced parental role but I deeply wanted a more hands-on relationship my sons. I was on the outside looking in at motherhood. Those invisible hands were again pushing me out of the lives of my loved ones. Pushing me out of life.

I worked extra hard to make up for being reduced in status by making great dinners and having family fun in the outdoors. In doing so, we built memories in new ways. But the ongoing disconnection between us during many of these activities was a continued threat. Even if I could not verbally communicate in a meaningful or effective way, we could at least spend time together shooting basketballs, hitting baseballs, camping, or going on vacation.

Anyone who has taken a youngster somewhere away from home knows the powerful connection that exists through each dip and curve of a rollercoaster, the crisp, clear splashes of ocean water, the bumpy abrasiveness of a bike ride in a big thicket, and the cheering crowd at a killer whale show. Just being there experiencing it together was very powerful and emotionally intense. We made the most of what we had, for as long as we could. I knew that each of my small offerings as a mother would eventually become a casualty of my growing disability. And "eventually" soon happened.

As I cooked dinner in the kitchen, my sons and I would attempt to converse while they did homework or watched TV in the living room. Even at close range using their loud voices, I could understand very little of their speech. And though lip reading the only option for me, it was a burden for them. How could they be expected to remain facing me while doing their homework or watching television? We tried very hard, but any connection we attempted to make was hindered by my inability to respond to their comments in a normal way at a normal speed.

Eventually they stopped talking to me before dinner, during homework time, and on movie nights. I had become a "Nevermind." This is the nickname I gave myself because I heard it so often when my sons grew tired of repeating themselves. "Nevermind" was a coping mechanism and provided them an escape from the frustration of having a disconnected mother—or to put it a nicer way, their way of letting me off the hook and allowing everyone to move on from a train wreck of a conversation. The frustration, distress, and panic that had been wearing me down was now wearing them down. As a result of many years of failed attempts to communicate effectively with my pre-teen sons and my increasingly intense panic attacks, our relationship eventually seemed to fade away.

Sadly, I didn't realize what I was losing until it was too late to save. 20/20 hindsight tells me that I should have integrated myself into the deaf community many decades before that point, forcing all of us to learn sign language as a way of connecting with one another. But as it was, we had no way to connect. I was on the brink of collapse because of all the mistakes I perceived myself to have made, mistakes that resulted in broken relationships.

Panic attacks were weekly by this time. Ray recognized the sharp decline in my hearing and personality but could do nothing but watch me sink. The boys watched uneasily as I struggled through each day, oftentimes becoming so frustrated I ended up in tears. One Saturday morning after a panic attack, I lay still and alone on the floor with a face salted with dried tears. Then a single lone ray of sunshine had slipped in through the window and rested on my hand.

> *Amazing grace, how sweet the sound,*
> *that saved a wretch like me!*
> *I once was lost but now am found,*
> *was blind but now I see!*

Inside that ray of light, I could see hope. I saw that I was not ready to give up yet— I was still hanging on. By the skin of my teeth. I didn't know it, but there was a miracle waiting to happen just around the corner.

As I lost touch with my sons, my relationship with my husband began to weaken as well, but not because I had become a "Nevermind." The dynamics between us at the time were confusing and emotional, pushing us to the limits. In the husband/ wife relationship of give and take, we were doing just that— giving and taking. But it was taking much more work than we had ever imagined. Ray gave of himself by taking on many of my responsibilities as a woman and mother.

He talked on the phone for me when I had to make appointments and such, translated for me when I could not hear friends and family speaking, ordered for me at restaurants, called the pediatrician when we had sick kids, called my doctor when I was sick, accompanied me to doctor appointments to hear for me, translated my voicemail, translated television shows that weren't captioned, went shopping with me to translate interactions with salespeople or cashiers, and attended parent conferences to translate for me. All the while, he kept his promise to me that he would not share my struggles with anyone. It was my challenge to overcome—and I wanted to do so privately. This amazing display of love should have been comforting.

Instead it sparked more panic attacks. Ironically, my initial appreciation and love shifted to ungratefulness and anger. It made no sense to either of us. But as I started to grasp the implications of his "help" I realized that I was losing my independence a little bit at a time. I blamed him because he was absorbing so much of my freedom.

With each bit of freedom that he unwittingly stole, he also snatched a chunk of my pride, and with that dangerous combination, resentment grew. I knew it was wrong. But I had to fight to keep from giving up. I pulled away to do my own things separate and independent from him—and discovered that the things I enjoyed most were done in solitude, where I didn't have to hear anything or anyone. I did only what I wanted to do, when I wanted to do it, on my own terms. In solitude, I was an independent woman and no one would be present to pass judgments.

I was so very tired of being in a world I could not fit into. Although my alone time was indeed lonely, it was also like a gift. If I couldn't have the hearing world, then I'd take the quiet one. Silence was the consolation prize.

Ray held up far better than me. He had his moments, but never abandoned his commitment to me, even when my emotions ran amok. I was filled with great sadness, frustration, resentment, and anger, and I needed an outlet for these emotions. Since I had stopped socializing, I had no support group. Sadly, this also effectively put an end to HIS social life as well because we had been a "couple" in everything we did. I had fallen into a hole again. But this time, as we grasped hands, instead of my husband pulling me out I was pulling him into the hole.

He insisted that the place he wanted to be was with me, whether it was at home or out and about. His strength did not have limits. I have always viewed my husband as a hero, ever since that first night when he drove two hours in the dark on his motorcycle to help me. But also because he continued to carry the weight of my disability, my struggles, and my emotions even through my darkest hour, which may well have been his darkest hour too.

We continued facing a growing list of challenges, and at the most perfect time, a gift was sent from Heaven—our first granddaughter, Elaina. We were in awe of her total perfection. Holding our little angel was a delightful, hopeful feeling. We welcomed this beautiful little promise of the future with joy and fell in love with her instantly.

I was disappointed but not surprised when I could not hear her coos as I held her. As a newborn, she did not care about my disability. There were plenty of smiles and snuggles to enjoy. Later on, her coos developed into babbling and when she began talking, our hearts overflowed with amazement. When we were lucky, her mother or father would put her on the phone to talk with us, and when that happened I was told that she babbled in the cutest way possible! How I longed to hear her voice! In my mind, she had the voice of an angel.

Experiencing this wonderful gift of our new little granddaughter and responding to her sweet attempts at communication is the stuff that every grandparent looks forward to. Instead I settled for the best I could get—Ray describing her cooing, babbling sounds, then helping me select appropriate verbal responses. I accepted this because I was absolutely going to take whatever I could get at this point—and was thankful for it. Shortly after Elaina's arrival, we discovered a second grand child would be arriving the following August! First rejoicing in the miracle, we then vowed to continue our team work in communicating. Elaina's birth brought to light our need to have a plan in place to help me to build a relationship with the grand children that I could not hear. Taia was born right on time and we were ready! Because of my incredibly patient, inclusive and loving step children, I did not miss any opportunities for hugs and kisses. Gratefully, I became a part of my grand children's lives. They called me Subie.

Shortly after her second birthday, my husband and I learned that Elaina would be coming to our home for a weeklong visit. We were so excited! When she and her parents arrived, we all sat together and watched this miraculous little creature playing with a puzzle on the floor. I hated to go to work the next day. I didn't want to miss a thing!

As I left for work the next morning, all I could think of was the joyful playtime awaiting us when I returned home that afternoon. I checked the clock repeatedly that day, looking forward to seeing her again, hugging her, and plopping down next to her with a little board book. After finishing my work, I pulled into the driveway and hurried out of my vehicle with great anticipation.

And there she was, sitting in her mother's lap at the kitchen table. She looked so precious! Cautiously, she studied me with her eyes open wide. It was almost as if she didn't remember me from the day before. Because she lived in a different city, there was always a moment of caution when we saw each other. As an educator, I know how important the "caution before kisses" moment is to a child's development of trust and love, and how detrimental an overbearing or forceful person can be to a child's sense of security and stability. So instead of picking her up, I sent her a smile and happy hello before continuing on to my bedroom to change clothes. When I opened the door, ready to head back into the kitchen, something stopped me dead in my tracks. My little granddaughter, that tiny angel, was silently staring up at me. Those big blue green eyes spoke to me, telling me that something was not right. I took her hand, and as we walked to the kitchen, I looked at her mother for answers.

My heart broke when she explained. My sweet little granddaughter had been trotting along behind me as I walked to my bedroom—calling out my name and reaching out for me. I never heard her. Even worse, just as she reached the doorway, I had shut the door in her face. Her mother told me she stood there and stared at the closed door.

This was one of the defining moments when I knew that my silent life simply was not acceptable. After everyone went to bed that night, I stayed up. It was near midnight when I took a walk outside, stopping at the end of the driveway. I was drawn to the full moon in the sky, comforted by its display of light and love. A star flickered nearby. Then the smaller stars that were spread out over the horizon caught my attention.

Throughout my life, I had viewed stars as the dreams I had for my life, past, present, and future. To me, that flickering star meant that it was time to pursue a big dream, a dream so big it would shine on over the remainder of my life. I knew what the dream was, but I had been too afraid to pursue it, fearing I would not be able to make it happen. I wanted to hear. I wanted relationships. I wanted life. In my mind, they were all bundled together and I was failing at them all.

A few weeks later, on the first day of spring, my husband and I sat in the stands watching my son's baseball game. This was his first year playing baseball so he had the least amount of experience of anyone on the team, but he rallied hard to improve. His performance during most games was good, but the amount of progress he showed each time he went out on the ball field was astonishing. This day, though, was the day he would really shine.

He got on base once, then twice, scoring the second time. I

cheered him on proudly and loudly. When my husband turned to the other parents on our team, I assumed he was talking to someone about the score since the scorekeeper had been making a few mistakes that day. I didn't take my eyes off the game because my son was having his best performance ever. Later on, near the end of the game, I asked my husband about his conversation with the other parents. "They were telling us how great Randy's doing and giving him all kinds of compliments!" he said.

Wait, they were saying wonderful things about my son—and I missed it? I felt like I'd been punched in the stomach. I'd missed it? I couldn't believe it! I'd missed out on hearing all the compliments about my sweet son. No! I couldn't accept it. This was as good as it gets? I would not only miss out on having conversations with my son, but also hearing the good things other people said about him? NO.

A volcano of frustration was building up inside me for the rest of the evening. At home that night, I decided that I needed some clean fresh air to rinse away my boiling anger. When I stepped outside, there it was, the thin white crescent hanging from above me. The sliver of the moon in the night sky looked almost like it was going to disappear altogether. And next to it was the flickering star again—the dream that was waiting to be chased.

The time was right. And I was ready. Looking up to the man in the moon, my old and trusted friend, I spoke to him. "I have had enough. I refuse to accept being on the outside of life looking in. There must be more." I was going to make my dream come true and that was that. I turned around, walked back inside, and opened up my laptop. It was time to jump hurdles and chase down the biggest, most important, and most unbelievable dream of my life.

XIII. HITTING THE JACKPOT

Jesus I don't understand
the reason for my sorrow
Oh my Lord, I beg for strength
to bravely face the 'morrow

—*S.L.*

2011

Late into the night, I worked my laptop into a heated frenzy, researching ideas, thoughts, views, and solutions for people like me, who were living a life on the outside looking in. Years of prayers, pleas, and struggles had prepared me for this long night. Never in any one of my prayers had I ever asked for a better set of circumstances. Instead I had been asking for an answer, a solution or a direction. As the early morning hours crept in, I sensed that I was getting closer to the answer.

Then I hit the jackpot. It had a name—and that name was Teri. As a "Hearing Loss Resource Specialist," how could this person not have an answer? Teri was hearing impaired herself and luckily, she was located in Houston. I needed to talk to her about how to keep from losing everything! My thoughts and feelings about the situation poured out of my fingers as if from a bucket full of tears, in an email to this woman I had found using a search engine on the Internet.

The very next morning, I received a response. Teri was a former teacher who had taken up teaching homebound students when she was no longer able to hear in a classroom setting. Most recently, she had taken a position as an advocate for hearing-impaired citizens. She made an appointment with me right away and I saw her two days later on a Saturday afternoon.

Teri listened to me that day, as I told her story after story of how my hearing loss had disconnected me from my family, friends, colleagues, and the rest of the world over the years. I told her how I had been cutting people off in mid-sentence without realizing it for many years, and although I hated the rudeness of it, I did not know how to prevent it from happening. I explained to Teri that my hearing aids continued to lose their effectiveness and this frightened me because they were the most powerful devices on the market. When I finished speaking, she asked me a question. "Have you looked into cochlear implants?"

My answer, that I did not qualify, was based on outdated information. Years before, maybe decades, I had investigated the cochlear implant, also known as the bionic ear, thinking it might help me. Through my research, I had discovered that I was not a candidate. But that was long ago—and I had never considered that the technology might have improved. And I felt it was far-fetched that someone who could hear would qualify—and even more important, that it would actually be covered by my insurance.

Teri invited me to a cochlear implant seminar coming up. And so I went, right along with my husband, who, of course, was there to hear for me. A funny thing happened at that seminar. I discovered that I probably was a candidate for a bionic ear, and that there was a very good possibility of my insurance covering the implant, so long as I followed the correct procedures and processes. One week later, I was sitting in an audiologist's office taking a hearing test conducted by a woman named Sherri. She recommended cochlear implants, although the doctor would be making the final decision. Then I walked across the street into the doctor's office for his official consultation. His recommendation? A cochlear implant in my right ear. Things began to move fast.

Two weeks after the hearing test and doctor recommendation, I had the implant surgery.

Things were moving even faster now, two weeks after the surgery, my implant was activated. This, as I wrote at the beginning of this book, was called "Activation Day," or "A-Day" for short. Although the official recommendation was to wait four to six weeks before being activated, I pleaded with the doctor, nurse, and anyone who would listen to activate me sooner than later. I wanted out of my quiet, isolated world! I am thankful that my doctor allowed the activation just two weeks after surgery. I was ready to leave behind a black-and-white world of silent solitude and step into the colorful world of sounds, voices, people, and music.

I was finally breaking out of my world and soaring right into theirs.

XIV. BACK TO THE FUTURE

Jesus Christ, I understand—
faith ought be my water.
Oh my Lord, to drink your love
tis strength that never falters!

—*S.L.*

MAY 18, 2011

*T*he daydream of life before the cochlear implant, as outlined in the last thirteen chapters, lasted no more than a few minutes—and ended as suddenly as it had begun with the voice of my audiologist asking if I had any other questions. With a blink, a sigh, and a smile, I realized that I had been deep in thought, savoring the most amazing moments of my life. It was important to understand the purpose they served so that the pieces would fit together.

I thanked Sherri for her role in the day's miracle, then told her that I was looking forward to becoming acquainted with sounds and would be relentless in my efforts to master them. Today was only the beginning. She expressed her support as well as some sound advice: that learning to hear again is a lifetime process. After nearly three hours, it had been a long hard day in her office—now it was time to walk away as a fully empowered, hearing woman. The ride home, as well as the rest of the evening, was filled with wondrous new sounds and surprises.

Although the day was coming to an end, I could not subdue my excitement. Later that evening, worn out from hearing, my body fell easily into bed but my eyes were wide open. I could not possibly sleep. I sat up, opened up my laptop, and began sending out notes to my friends on my favorite social network, updating them of the day's events and responding to emails from excited family, friends, and colleagues. This was the best day of my life!

Over the next week, I was showered with gifts of sound. Some sounds I found absolutely shocking—such as locusts, water running, markers squeaking, and hearing myself talking to myself. These sounds were so unexpected that it took some time before I was altogether accustomed to them. Other sounds I found completely hysterical, such as voices. They sounded like a cross between a chipmunk and a robot. I didn't always explain my private laugh to others since I quite enjoyed all the interesting reactions to my giggles. Laughing out loud as other people spoke sent them checking for toilet tissue on their shoes or mucus in their noses.

There were a few other sounds that turned me into a giggle box as I was learning to live in my new world, such as crickets, a man snoring, and the whines of our 160-pound dog. And then there were the sounds that touched me with such intensity they brought chills to my skin, warmth to my heart, and sometimes tears to my eyes.

The first was hearing my son's voice—I mean really hearing it and not just small pieces of it—for the first time since he was about six years old. It was a moment to remember. I couldn't believe how much he did not sound like the little boy I remembered. His voice had been changing as he grew through the years while I had been losing my hearing. It was a strange feeling to hear my son's voice but not recognize it.

I was very motivated to work on learning and listening to his voice. I am also sure he was none too happy to have me stalking him for conversation. Regardless of the hassles it posed, both of us were aware that hearing his voice was the connection we had been lacking for several years.

The second memorable moment occurred while I was at school doing something I had done hundreds of times: working with kids. A certain little pre-kindergartener did something she had done many times before: she got off her bus and walked toward me with a smile. This child's smile was always accompanied by a merry little comment, which I never responded to, although she always received a smile in return as well as a warm hug for good measure.

But this morning, when she spoke her merry little words, I heard them for the first time. "Do you like my new boots?" she asked. With a great big smile, I responded, "I love your new boots, almost as much as I love you."

And there was the day I heard my husband and son singing happy birthday to me at the strike of midnight on my birthday, then hearing my cousin Rebecca singing a beautiful version of the happy birthday song in a voicemail message. Though I had probably heard the happy birthday song hundreds if not thousands of times, this time it was the sweetest song I ever heard, because of the love in those three voices.

Funny sounds, sweet sounds, birthday songs, and children's voices — I felt as though I was living Side A of a hit record! Gratitude and appreciation will always run deep in my veins because personal memories will always remind me of a time when I was living Side B.

XV. DEAR DIARY

A word is worth a thousand kisses.
Words touching tenderly,
connecting two souls,
cozy, contented sharing—
intimate, reciprocal.

—S.L.

What follows are the first two months of the notes I took as my cochlear implant experience unfolded. I recorded most of these moments on poster boards, creating a living diary in order to capture as much of the magic as I could. Mixed in with the poster board entries are entries from my social network and blog posts from the Cochlear Community.

MAY 18, 2011—ACTIVATION DAY, POSTER DIARY

Dear Diary, this is the best day of my life.

I am the proud owner of a new bionic ear! The activation went pretty well! The new sounds are daunting and breathtaking at the same time. I am so happy that it worked, most of all. My deepest, darkest fear was that it wouldn't work and I'm not sure I would have bounced back from that kind of a disaster. But it DID work. It was a long afternoon, but full of new things, starting with the ride home.

The blinker—it doesn't actually blink— it CLICKS. I will now be the one reminding THEM to turn the turn indicator off.

Keys jingling—this phrase is a polite way of saying the keys were clanking about like pennies in a tin can.

Birds—they don't sing, they chirp. My

157

backyard sounds like a jungle!

The microwave—it beeps four times. I will never burn popcorn again!

Spoons—they clank, and lots of times when dropped! What a painful sound, as if the spoon is actually screaming at me for dropping it!

I walked around the house several times, just listening. I can hear the air conditioner on and the doors closing all around the house. I can hear my son's video game from outside his bedroom.

I can't understand speech yet, even though I can hear voices. Speech is made up of so many sounds! Household noises are very short and repetitious, making it much easier to train my brain.

Saying goodnight and hearing "good night" in return felt so good, and sounded good too!

I can hear so much! Identifying each new sound is going to take a while but it is worth the wait, and it's worth the work I will have to put into it.

I am worn out!

Tomorrow brings a new day, a new experience, and a new joy in my new life.

MAY 19, 2011, POSTER DIARY

Voices are now voices—well almost! But they continue to favor R2D2.

I hope those around me don't notice me laughing under my breath, but it's just funny! It's hard to identify who is who by the sound of their voice, but in time I am certain there will be a marked difference I the way I "hear" each voice.

Went online to report the news of my bionic ear to friends and had another cochlear implant moment—the fast and furious tap-tap-tapping of the keys on this keyboard makes it sound as if the words themselves are running from me—in high heels—right into the screen.

This is the best day of my life!

MAY 20 BLOG

I noticed this morning that there were numerous sounds. There many things I had been missing.

The security scanner beeped when I scanned my card—a very high pitched and faint beep. Nice! This is a sound I NEVER could have imagine existed.

Then in my classroom, my eraser made an odd noise as I rubbed it along the paper, back and forth. I did it a few extra times just for fun.

I was able to hear people wearing noisy shoes walking up behind me, which is kind of cool. I really wanted to swing around and yell BOO!

I can still hear my keys. But they are getting irritating.

Ah, the sweet delicate sounds of wine pouring like a gentle waterfall into a glass.

I must be sure not to ruin it with a "gulp."

Another adventurous day in your world. Thanks for having me, world! This is the best day of my life!

MAY 21, , POSTER DIARY

Experienced the sound of a fire alarm at work today. It's such a horrible sound—yet beautiful! It could save the lives of our students!

Now I understand why everyone rushes out from the building as fast as humanly possible. They are trying to get as far away from the screeching alarm as fast as they can.

Took a ride on the bike trail with my husband this evening and heard all kinds of birds, chirps, crickets. It sounded like we were riding through the Amazon jungle. It was the best day of my life!

MAY 22, , POSTER DIARY

Wolfgang (our dog) is a big old bear! He pants like a bear might pant too. He can only stand being outside long enough to do his business because of the heat, so when he's out there much longer, he cries. Poor, poor doggy! I can let him in when he cries now— because I can hear him! I love you, Wolfgang!

Heard the intermittent sound of cicadas this evening—and although I carefully observed the trees and bushes, I could not find a single one!

Chicken sizzling! Oh my Heavens! The chicken on

the grill popped and crackled, adding some zip to an otherwise dull task. Who knew grilling chicken could sound as good as it smelled? This is the best day of my life!

MAY 23, , POSTER DIARY

This morning I heard my husband showering while I was in another room! It seems like I can always figure out where he's in the house, now that I can track his movement through the recognizable noises! It is marvelous to not feel alone in a house full of people.

At work today, I heard what I would call a squeak, although I am unsure what a squeak sounds like in the first place. But let's call it a squeak. It was coming from my marker as I wrote on my whiteboard during a lesson with my third-graders. I jumped out of my chair, looking all around my office, and trying to locate the origin of the squeak. But it had stopped. My students looked around as well, following my lead. Not knowing where the squeak was coming from, I resumed writing. And there it was again!

Now I had figured it out! It was coming from my marker as I moved it across the whiteboard. I said "oh my gosh!" and my students laughed and cheered. It was a great way to start the day.

Then later on, after lunchtime, another new sound—definitely a surprising sound. And one I hope to someday forget. The burp. The first one made a revolting noise, followed by another. Each one had a personality of its own. This is one of the very few downsides of being able to hear everything—kid burps. I can't even imagine a

full-grown adult burp—and, actually, I don't want to.
Lord protect me.

MAY 24, BLOG

Voices continue to sound like Mr. and Mrs. Robot, but as each day goes by, my brain interprets them a little more humanly.

This afternoon, as I sat in my classroom thinking, I began speaking to myself. I have been told for years that I do it all the time, but I never believed it. And here I was, having a conversation with myself. When the school secretary walked in, she caught me laughing—so I explained that I had just discovered the conversations I had with myself.

She laughed out loud too, telling me that she had noticed, the teachers had noticed, the kids had noticed and administrators had noticed. The only one who hadn't noticed was me, until now. It never bothered them at all—they just accepted it as part of who I was. I feel so grateful for the acceptance and understanding of so many of my colleagues.

Just before school let out this afternoon, a child was walking through the chaos and noise to her daycare line. She stopped as she reached me and tugged at my shirt. As I looked down at her, she asked, "Can I go to the bathroom?"

"Yes," I told her, "but go quickly and be careful." As she hurried away, my eyes popped out of my head. I HEARD HER!

This was a huge achievement and made me want to say "Thank you Lord!" right there on the spot. So I did. I whispered it to myself, although it probably went unheard because of the noise that nine hundred children make as they are being released from school.

MAY 25, SOCIAL NETWORK

This morning someone honked at me. Three times! This is the best day of my life! I smiled my biggest smile as she passed by me honking, and waved at her happily. It was not a Texas honk though, and certainly not what I imagined a honk would sound like. It was more of a toot. But it was the sweetest toot I ever knew! I was told later this afternoon by an SUV owner that they don't make horns the way they used to.

Voices continue to become more human—like the voices of teachers, students and friends.

Heard Wolfgang whining again tonight—he wanted to come into the living room and sit with us on the couch. Such a sad little sound coming from a huge, lovable beast. I gave him a pat on his head, but didn't let him sit with us. If we allowed him to do that, he would break our legs.

MAY 26, POSTER DIARY

Today was a loud day. I am starting to need a break from the noise in this world.

This evening, Ray and I biked up to the Waterway, testing it to see if my bionic ear would stay secure the whole ride up. It passed the test.

We had frozen yogurt, and I ordered it myself. Then we walked up and down the Waterway, eating our yogurt, talking at length, and enjoying each other. Have I been missing this all my life? Relationships have always been so hard—and now it's so easy!

Relationships can grow through walks, talks, and frozen yogurt.

These are the best days of my life.

MAY 27, POSTER DIARY

My pen rolled horizontally across the table, making a great sound as it did so. I enjoyed it so much I childishly rolled it about ten more times. I just can't get enough of these incredible sounds! I feel like a kid who's been let out of a closet and is living life for the first time. It's miraculous. Pure magic!

Turned on the truck stereo to a rock and roll music station, preparing myself for Randy's orchestra concert tonight. I still hear music and songs in my head, but it sounds nothing like the way I hear it with my implant. I listened to the rock and roll for about fifteen minutes, then it was time to rest. Sometimes it's too odd to figure out.

Tonight was the big night: Randy's concert. I heard

lots of different instruments, including the treble sounds I had lost long ago. What I cannot do yet is recognize which sound goes with its corresponding instrument. I need to give it some practice. In time, my brain will be programmed to interpret the instruments correctly. But seeing him play his violin tonight, having the ability to follow the music—and especially learning how to hear the violin—was a priceless connection. It was the best day of my life!

MAY 28, SOCIAL NETWORK

Independence Day—I ordered my lunch at a restaurant ON MY OWN. Why?

Because I can!

No translating.

No repeating.

No mistakes!

This is the best day of my life!

I have the whole thing memorized.

Waitress: Are you ready to order, ma'am?

Me: Why yes, I am!

Waitress: Okay! Go ahead.

Me: I will have the fish tacos, please!

Waitress: Grilled shrimp, grilled cod, fried cod, or one of each?

Me: One of each, please!

Waitress: Corn or flour tortilla?

Me: Corn, please!

Waitress: Red sauce and green sauce?

Me: Yep!

Just one month ago, all these questions from

the waitress would have been a disaster.

MAY 29, SOCIAL NETWORK

I am hearing raindrops falling on the windowpanes for the first time. How amazingly delicate and musical! This is the best day of my life!

MAY 30, POSTER DIARY

I made HUGE progress on my listening training tests. I scored over 90% on almost all of the tests, except music and hearing sentences in noisy environments. All in due time.

Ironically, just a few hours after feeling like a highfalutin overachiever, I was put back into my place. Having a little bit of quiet time, I sat in my big blue easy chair clicking away on my laptop, chatting online with friends about my amazing test scores from earlier in the day. Suddenly a long, loud buzz overcame the entire house. It was very abrupt and coarse, and I held my breath until it was over. My heart began to pound, and I felt a panic coming on. PANIC—it was such a familiar feeling and one that I thought had disappeared forever! What was this hideous noise?

Thinking it might be a federal warning of a terror attack, I rushed to the window and peeked outside. It was dark, but quiet. None of the neighbors were even out. It was as if nothing ever happened. So I walked back inside, sat down on my easy chair, took a deep breath, and waited, wondering if it would happen again. And it did. This time I could feel tears coming down. I was so scared, but too proud to call my husband and ask him to explain the sound.

This time I concluded that the sound was the fire alarm. I quickly walked from room to room, sniffing the air for traces of smoke. After having walked almost through the entire house without spotting any smoke or fire, I stopped in the laundry room just before I marched out the door.

Then it happened again, this time so loud and harsh the ground vibrated, as if the sound were right upon me. I screamed and grabbed onto the nearest stationary object—the dryer. It was vibrating at exactly the same pace as the sound.

THE DRYER? REALLY? Really.

It was the dryer. How had I gone for so long not hearing such a horrifying loud buzzer? It was an eye opener, that was for certain. I realized how little I had been hearing before the implant, and I also realized how much I COULD hear with the bionic ear. WOW.

I felt slightly dizzy, and went to bed earlier than usual. Life is such an adventure!

MAY 31, BLOG

It's two weeks post activation. I love the journey of learning how to hear.

There is one small distraction, however. I have become dizzy. Not as in ditzy dizzy. Dizzy dizzy. The kind where my head sort of spins and I lose my balance a bit—but not enough to fall over like a drunk. It's odd and annoying.

If I'd had this dizziness since I got the implant, as other recipients have mentioned, I would simply be waiting for it to fade away. But my dizziness didn't start until ten days after activation. Having waited four days to mention it, I am ready to whine about it. I will ask my implant friends from the Cochlear Community for their thoughts.

On the upside, this morning I heard several kids' voices in a noisy hallway—sure do hope I am learning how to filter out all the background noise and zoom in on voices!

JUNE 1, BLOG

Today I called the doctor about the dizziness. He said exactly what I thought he would—dizziness is normal and it happens in some people. There is nothing to be concerned about because of the absence of fever, pain, or bleeding.

I adjusted the sensitivity setting as a friend had suggested because late last week, the sound coming from my implant suddenly became intense, almost harsh. It was happening about the same time I was feeling dizzy, and then nauseated. Lowering the sensitivity helped a tad, but the sound was still very intense, even on a lower sensitivity, if that makes sense.

I just sat in my big ol' easy chair and thought about what could be causing my dizziness. Thought and thought and thought—and I came up with nothing! It was so frustrating that I took the whole thing off, and held it up in front of my face while staring at it. As if this whole dizzy problem weren't kooky enough, now I was talking to my processor (the external part of the device)."Why are you doing this?" There was no reply so I added, "WELL, that's not very nice, you know."

As I finished my sentence, something caught my eye. I spied a tiny little hole in a place where a hole was not supposed be! Upon further inspection, I discovered something else—the little microphone was fully exposed. Its little cover had come off. The microphone was naked! Everything else on the processor was perfect. I don't know how or when or why, but something had knocked the microphone cover off.

I examined it very, very closely, holding it within inches of my eyes as if I were a scientist studying a DNA sample through a powerful microscope. Then I jumped up, dashed over to my closet and pulled out my Cochlear Americas suitcase. Piece by piece, box by box, I searched for something I did not know the name of, only that I needed it.

MICROPHONE COVERS.

That's it! I grabbed the box and ran back to my chair, where my processor was waiting. Dr. Suzie to the rescue. I would be implanting a microphone cover right on my processor. WOW—I was implanting my implant! I was very nervous as I started the procedure, but the end result was quite impressive as the sound changed immediately—smoother and softer.

I can't say that it's a tender, warm, fuzzy sound yet because I'm in such a strange new world. But, I love the adventure of being here, in their world, which I think is now mine. The dizziness started to subside within an hour of replacing the microphone cover, and had all but disappeared by bedtime.

JUNE 2, POSTER DIARY

Voices sound like voices now—robots have left the room!

JUNE 3, POSTER DIARY

I looked at my calendar this morning and noticed that Ray and I had a lunch date with our dear friends Chuck and Shirin. It was my first lunch date with another couple in a long time and I hoped to be actively engaged, enjoying myself, not wishing I could hide under the table. We decided to meet them at the restaurant because I was not ready to ride over with them. Car rides have been extremely stressful over the years and I didn't want to start the afternoon on a tense note.

We went for Chinese food, sat at a round table, smiled, greeted each other—and then watched each other cautiously. We were all wondering about my bionic ear! When Shirin asked me how my cochlear implant was doing, I knew it was working. Without a doubt, I had heard every word she asked without looking at her lips! And I did this in a restaurant setting! We had a great lunch together celebrating our friendship. It was the best day of my life!

JUNE 4, POSTER DIARY

Today at the beach, I heard the lifeguard blowing his whistle at a man in the water. I kept my eye on the man swimming in the ocean—what if he can't hear? The lifeguard was blowing the whistle over and over, trying to get his attention. After several minutes, the man came back in. The sound of the whistle makes me think about everything I was missing, even the safety alerts. I was so relieved the man was safe.

JUNE 5, POSTER DIARY

Tried listening to music again—still not what I am hoping for because I haven't figured out all the instruments. I have been told that music just sounds differently with a bionic ear. How can I complain, though, when I can hear all the high-pitched parts of music that I have never heard before?

JUNE 6, POSTER DIARY

Today was the last day of school. But this time I didn't avoid people, which had been a lifelong habit stemming from isolation and mistrust. This time there were lots of hugs and goodbyes. These were authentic connections. It was the best "last day of school" of my life.

JUNE 7, POSTER DIARY

Ran five miles on the elliptical while watching TV as I was sweating it up. It was the best run of my life!

Being able to watch TV and actually hear it makes a huge difference when I use the exercise machine. I can't believe I ever jogged on these machines without listening to music or watching TV! So boring!

JUNE 8, POSTER DIARY

Today my husband and I made the three-hour drive with my son to meet his dad—my son sat in front; I was in back. I didn't have my implant set correctly for optimum performance in a vehicle, so the ride was not what I thought it would be. I couldn't hear him talking from the back seat—all I could hear was the motor humming. I hoped the ride home with him in four weeks would be better.

After dropping my son off, my husband and I went on a road trip to Austin. There, I checked in to the hotel myself, without making mistakes, without help, or even wishing I had some help! Being independent is so liberating and empowering. This is the best day of my life!

JUNE 9, POSTER DIARY

Motorcycle ride through the hill country! I was in pain for most of the morning because my helmet was putting a great deal of pressure on my implant. The whole area was throbbing. When the pain became unbearable, I pulled into a gas station almost in tears. I could not imagine having to give up my motorcycle rides but the stinging pain was impossible. After pinpointing the exact location of the pain behind my ear and matching it to the inside of the helmet, he took out his doctor bag and got to work. With his scalpel, he performed surgery on my helmet, removing a huge chunk of padding from the inside of my helmet. When the operation was over, he passed the helmet back to me, saying, "Let's give it a try."

Tensely, I placed the helmet over my head. I closed my eyes and focused on my head ... my helmet ... my feelings ... myself.

No pain! None at all! My husband is the best helmet doctor in the world. We rode for a few more hours. I am free, so free!

This is the best day of my life!

JUNE 10, POSTER DIARY

We are enjoying our motorcycle trip though the hill country today and had dinner at a delicious restaurant, a very noisy, crowded Mexican place. I was nervous. But I am SO tired of being nervous and I'm tired of being stressed about being alive. I am in their world now.

They have accepted it, but now I have to accept it! I am no less capable than any hearing person, although I am still learning new sounds. So I took a walk on the wild side and decided to order myself, amid the boisterous, college-age crowd of hungry patrons.

My remote setting was on the Focus program, zooming in on one person's voice. So when the waitress came for our order, it zoomed in on HER voice. Amazingly, I did hear her! I ordered fajitas, a margarita for each of us, another margarita for each of us, and then asked for the check. SO cool!

This is the best day of my life!

JUNE 11, POSTER DIARY

Today was so hot! I heard Wolfgang was panting loudly for a good part of the day. He must really get hot in the furry coat he wears all day long. Practiced my Sound and Way Beyond DVD and did okay. I have slacked off a bit and now feel that I am losing some ground. I need to push myself to keep learning how to hear. It's a lifelong process, not an overnight miracle.

JUNE 12 , POSTER DIARY

Another cochlear implant moment! Tonight as I was boiling water to make spaghetti, I realized I was hearing the water boil. Blup, blup, blup, blup, blup. Sounds like someone is drowning down there in the pot! Voices are sounding better; this must be another turning point. Yay!

JUNE 13, POSTER DIARY

We are on our way to go biking on the seawall in Galveston for the weekend. I am nervous about being around saltwater for two straight days, with my processor on. Although it's water resistant, I am unclear about its resistance to salt. I researched it as best I could, but came up with nothing to indicate that salt would damage the processor.

So here I am, writing in my diary on the beach in Galveston—wearing my processor, but worried about it! Because I don't ever want to go back to the world I came from, I will be hyper protective of my bionic ear.

Music—I'm not able to fully appreciate it yet, but still trying!

Spent half the night in the truck parked on the seawall watching the stars twinkle and the full moon shine on the ocean below. I had my processor on as I listened to the waves gently crashing. Peace. Joy. Life. This is the best night of my life.

JUNE 14 BLOG

Preparing for my third mapping tomorrow, doing quite a bit of sound testing and practice. So nervous—but hoping it goes well and that I am still improving! I haven't even realized that I am, without a doubt, improving. There have been subtle improvements in my capabilities—such as this evening when I had a pleasant, although short, conversation with Randy. Why was it a big deal? He was in the living room talking and I was in the kitchen listening, hearing—and responding! It was a two-way conversation.

I am no longer a Nevermind.

This is such an amazing grace. And this is the best day of my life!

JUNE 15, BLOG

For four weeks, I have been trying my best to improve my ability to hear with my bionic ear accomplishments. The first mapping went well enough, although it was almost painful to hear all the screeches and whistles. I had been told what to expect, and that it would be hard work—but secretly I thought I would be different, that it would be a cakewalk for me because—well, because I am special. I felt special all right—and naïve—to think I could skip all the groundwork.

The second mapping went better, because I was actually able to hear a voice in all the noise somewhere. I had used my Sounds and Way Beyond DVD as much as I could to accelerate my learning. Now I was ready for the third mapping. It was another nervous day as I wondered if I would perform as well as I wanted to. This was important. I needed to know that I was, in fact, learning to hear!

As my audiologist Sherri fine-tuned the electrodes and balanced them out, everything all came together yet AGAIN, this time even more so than the last two mappings. I realized that all the remaining noises from before had now become sounds—the sounds that made up words! It was so exciting! I felt a confidence within—the kind I don't ever remember feeling. And I felt like I could make it in this hearing world. Only those with cochlear implants can understand this feeling—it is ours.

The next part of my hearing test was to assess how well I could understand sentences. On my second mapping, my score was a meager 17%, meaning I could only hear seventeen words out of a hundred. But I was told that 17% was better than most implant users could manage at that stage.

Truthfully, I think I guessed correctly on the 17% and didn't really earn it. I didn't remember hearing much of anything. I was SO nervous about this! During the practice piece, I told Sherri that the volume seemed much too low. As always, she said to do the best I can. Despite my concerns, I DID hear—and I also scored 89% on the third mapping! I guess I CAN hear.

All the worries about my progress, and all the jittery nerves—why do I continue putting myself through this? Way back before the surgery, I was given some important advice—"trust the process." At that time, I did not understand what it meant, so I tortured myself trying to skip the process! Now I understand.

JUNE 16, POSTER DIARY

So excited! I can hear, I can hear, I can HEAR HEAR HEAR!

I spent the day looking for people to talk to—in stores, with neighbors and total strangers—wondering if I am the irritating type now—the kind you wish would just hush! But not me, I am not hushing. I will never be hushed again. Oh, Mom, I am missing you—looking forward to having a conversation without having to guess what you are saying. I want to hear your real voice soon, not the muffled crackly junk I have been hearing for so long.

JUNE 17, POSTER DIARY

Went bike riding down to Market Street, hearing all the glorious sounds along the way. I am so thankful to be in their world—I mean MY world. Why didn't I have the surgery sooner? I am going to help other profoundly hearing-impaired people find their way to cochlear implants—the same way I had been determined to help hearing-impaired children be identified in schools. And I am starting right NOW!

JUNE 18, BLOG AND SOCIAL NETWORK

Pool party—I was incredibly worried. My heart tells me that I'm not ready, but I'm so tired of being afraid to live. I can do this, I will do this, and I must do this.

Moreover, it's important to Ray. He has missed out on so many social events over the years, staying home with someone who was too disconnected and troubled to enjoy people—of course, that someone is me. He has never ever complained. I love and admire you so much, Ray. So this pool party is my gift to you.

Here we go. It was a pool party, all right. And it was drenched in disaster. After five weeks of hearing new sounds, gaining voice comprehension in small-group conversations during strategic outings, and lots of exciting bionic moments, yesterday the felt like two steps back.

This was a party I probably should have skipped, but I wanted to try. After all, it was my husband's group of friends, and he has missed MANY social opportunities or had them cut short because of his concern that I was unable to communicate with his world. My intention was for this gift to wow him! Unlike times in the past when I could hear very little and sat smiling in silence while the rest of the world communicated, this event was quite different. However, the outcome still ended up the same.

I did hear this time. I heard the music in the background blaring in my ear through what must have been fifteen speakers mounted all over the backyard. I heard the men blabbing, the women yapping, the water splashing, the door opening and closing. I heard the people playing water volleyball wahooing and yahooing, the wind blowing in my ear, and someone dragging a chair around on the pavement.

Among all those sounds, which I will call noises for all practical purposes; I could NOT capture a single person's voice. In less than an hour, I was frustrated and fatigued. I moved around the party several times, trying to find just the right angle for optimal hearing. I tried out several different programs on my remote control for the best fit. I took a short walk down the street to regroup, hoping another idea would pop into my mind and possibly save the day.

Unfortunately, it was not to be. It was too much, too soon. I wasn't ready. I had rushed the process. Now I have the tasty opportunity to eat the words "trust the process." This is the idea I have been lecturing to my friends who've recently had cochlear implants. They are precisely the words I need to grab hold of right away.

Trust the process. It means: have faith, work hard, and not give up, and everything will fall into place. Eating those words, and digesting their meaning will be good for me. I listened to the birds, had a very nice conversation with my husband, sang in the kitchen, and enjoyed all the sounds I have been hearing for a month now. For all of those, I am truly thankful. The next pool party will be in my bathtub and I am the only one who is invited.

JUNE 19, SOCIAL NETWORK

I am not a shopper. It's practically torture. But shop I did this afternoon for a few hours, at an outdoor clothing and accessory store. Even better, they were having a "Blowout Sale". What was the BEST THING? When I tried on a few items, I heard the attendant ask me if I was doing okay—and the fitting room door was completely

CLOSED! I HAD to tell her the truth: this is the best day of my life!

After shopping—we had dinner on the backyard deck—also known as the jungle. Those amazing birds, frogs, cicadas, and crickets! I felt like I was in an exotic movie preparing to dine with Tarzan. I am so happy and content.

JUNE 20, POSTER DIARY

Today I am going for a manicure. I have stayed far, far away from these kinds of places in the past—being unable to communicate with the employees made it useless for me to be there. These are the types of settings where, no matter how many times they repeat themselves, I would never have been able to figure out what they are saying. Until now, the vocabulary, dialect, and accent of Asians have always been an obstacle. I pulled into the parking lot then put the gear in park, leaving the engine running. With the disastrous pool party still on my mind, I placed the gear back into drive and went home. I chickened out of getting the manicure. Maybe I'll try another time.

JUNE 21, POSTER DIARY

Ta-dah!

I had another room-to-room conversation, this time with Ray. How odd to be talking to him and not to even be looking at him, or even more bizarre—to not even be in the SAME ROOM with him? When it happened, he walked into the room where I was and looked completely stunned. "You heard me!" he said. Then he smiled a great big smile. I am equal with Ray. I love his world. I love my world. I love OUR world. This is the best day of my life!

JUNE 22, POSTER DIARY

Dear Diary, I lost the remote control to my cochlear implant today. I am going to keep quiet and hope it turns up.

JUNE 23, POSTER DIARY

I love going out to eat!

There are so many restaurants, so few hours in the day. Dining out is such fun when you can have great conversations along with great food. I can't believe I hated eating out for so long and sure hope I don't get too big for my britches, literally.

JUNE 24, POSTER DIARY

Fun times! We went out to Sonic at almost midnight for an ice cream run. I just love eating out! We had fun, silly conversations at Sonic while we ate our ice cream— and I didn't have to stop eating so I could read Ray's lips during the conversation. I pigged out freely, and hogged the conversation too! It was the best day of my life!

JUNE 25, POSTER DIARY

We ate out again. Oh how I love eating out!

Margaritas at a Mexican restaurant made for a nice cool afternoon with a long talk about our retirement plans. I plan to eat out when I retire.

JUNE 26, POSTER DIARY

We had dinner with our neighbors Ralph and Rhonda, in their home. I am no longer afraid to go into other's people's houses. We are so happy to spend the evening with them because I never had a chance to really get to know them until now. Missed so many chances because I was a coward and could not tell anyone how needy I was.

But what was I to do? What was ANYONE to do? I thank God I have found my place. We had such a great time tonight—words are like kisses between kindred spirits. With my husband and neighbors, I am building a real connection through hearing, speech and language.

A KISS
Lips touching tenderly
connecting two souls.
Cozy contented sharing,
intimate and reciprocal.

A CONVERSATION
Words touching tenderly
connecting two souls.
Cozy, contented sharing,
intimate and reciprocal.

JUNE 27, POSTER DIARY

We are painting the interior of the house. I painted all afternoon as I sang and whispered to myself. I still can't believe I can hear myself singing and whispering. Funny—I've been doing it all my life and never ever knew how loud I sing and that my personal debates have been completely audible!

JUNE 28, POSTER DIARY and SOCIAL NETWORK

Painted again all day long. Then attended a staff development all afternoon. I felt like everyone was talking to me at once! During the workshop, two people were talking to me at the same time. Is this a normal thing for people to do? I couldn't hear either one of them. Even worse was just before the Meet and Greet part of the workshop, which sounded like twenty-two people were all talking to me at once.

It was a minor setback because each voice I heard was so loud and yet I couldn't pull in a specific voice when I wanted to. I need to learn how to FOCUS on the person I want to hear because hearing twenty-two people at once is just as useless as hearing NOTHING.

JUNE 29, BLOG

This is the best day of my life! I said the same thing yesterday—and the day before that as well. Truth is, I have been saying it for years. It's a fact—I do say today is the best day almost every single day. And it's a statement that prompts my son to roll his eyes and laugh. He doesn't know that he is one of the reasons that every day is the best day of my life. My husband does not know that he is another reason.

The sun coming up ... the smell of pancakes ... praying at the dinner table ... a child giggling ... a colorful flower ... the wind in my hair ... a date with my boyfriend (who also happens to be my husband) ... a date with my son ... cooking for my family ... singing in the kitchen...

Now that I can hear the list goes on and on and on, filled with things that bless me with another best day of my life. I do have my share of issues and sadness, but when I am a hundred years old and on my deathbed, I don't think I am going to say "Gee, I wish I could have worried a little bit more."

My cochlear implant has gifted me with hearing. Hearing has gifted me with new joys—and more reasons to have the best day of my life, today and always.

JUNE 30, POSTER DIARY

I had a cochlear implant moment while I was painting, when I heard a drop of paint drip on the drop cloth.

Such a gentle little sound, but it was gigantic to me because I heard it in the first place. And to have heard it while I was standing on a ladder was colossal!

Maybe I was mistaken? I wanted to be sure. So I purposefully let a small drop of paint drip down on the drop cloth from atop the ladder once again. What I heard was, in fact, the sound of a drop! The kid in me wanted to drip a drop again and again, sort of like playing with elevator buttons. But the rational adult buried somewhere inside of me took charge and saved the paint—and probably the rug too.

THE AMAZING RIDE HOME

This afternoon I picked Randy up in Corsicana for the long ride home. No sooner had he buckled up did we jump right into a highly spirited, blissful conversation. We talked about so many things—mostly about topics that he initiated. Hearing him was so easy and the words flowed sweetly and easily between us like lemonade from pitcher, quenching our thirst to reach each other. What a reunion we had! The ride home seemed to last only seconds. The three of us were in total harmony—all due to my bionic ear being set on the correct programming.

The connection I felt with my incredibly funny and loving son was a gift worth waiting for, and a long time coming. I am in his world at last.

It was the best day of my life!

JULY 1, POSTER DIARY

I woke up this morning and forgot to put my

processor on right away. Then I walked around the house, noticing how strange everything seemed. So quiet. So dead. So blah. It's scary how little I can hear! Switching the processor on still shocks me momentarily every morning—loud and crispy like a hyperactive "good morning" greeting from a robot in my head.

JULY 2, POSTER DIARY

For years I have been enjoying my adult step son Ryan's music to the best of my ability—lots of bass and some melody.

His latest CD, I was told, was very distinctive because of his band's new sound. From what I could hear of it, the music was not bad. But it sounded like it was missing something. And it was. What I had been hearing before the implant was a small piece of his music, not its full body and passion. Today, though, I heard Ryan's music! Just like he says, it is toe-tapping, knee-slapping entertainment.

Ryan is powerful motivation to learn how to hear and appreciate music now that I can hear his songs. And I have shown considerable improvement, evidenced by my ability to hear, tap, and slap to the music!

JULY 3, POSTER DIARY

I experienced FREEDOM tonight! Heading to the pavilion for the Independence Day concert, my only hope was to hear the 1812 Overture in its entirety. I had heard it many times over, but only heard portions of it—

the cannons, drums, bass, and some trumpet, I think.

However, now I can hear much more. And although I am not sure what instrument matches each sound, I watched very closely! Amazingly, I heard most of the 1812 Overture! The sounds I did not recognize, I will continue to study. But I know for certain that there is so much more to this special piece of music than just drums, bass, and cannons!

The other song I was hoping to experience was Sousa's "Stars and Stripes Forever." I've heard it in my head since experiencing it live for the first time when I was eleven years old in 1976, the year of America's two hundredth birthday celebration. My dad loved the song, turning it up full volume so the entire family could experience history in the passion of the music, including the climactic cannons at the end. Back then I could hear fairly well when the music was loud enough. I was able to capture some of the flute sections as well as the wonderful melody. I have loved "Stars and Stripes Forever" since then. But I haven't heard it as fully or richly as I did when I was eleven. I was so excited about hearing it this evening!

When I sat down on the lawn and read over the program, I noticed that Sousa was not on it. I was shocked. All through the concert I mumbled how I could not believe that the song had been left out on Independence Day. I was hugely disappointed.

Later on in the evening, an astronaut came onstage and sang a song he had written about going into space, and what it meant to be an American. It was a poignant song, and that moment was enough to replace any disappointment with by grace and gratitude for living in America where I was able to have the cochlear implant and finally be able to hear again.

When the concert ended, I rose for the standing ovation and began packing up my things. Then it happened. Encore! Sousa's "Stars and Stripes Forever"! As the symphony began their surprising encore, a flag spanning the full length of the stage began slowly rolling down from the ceiling. I was completely overcome as the huge American flag and John Philip Sousa grabbed my heart.

It was a fabulous surprise ending. And the flutes that I heard were better than I remembered from 1976! I am so lucky to have had my hearing restored, even though I am deaf. It is such a miracle! Tonight was the best night of my life. Dad, I know you are beaming proudly from somewhere in the stars.

JULY 4 , POSTER DIARY

I can't get enough patriotic music—I listened to it all evening on television. Independence Day programs were broadcast live on the East Coast, the West Coast and the Gulf Coast too! Each time I listened to a song for a second time, I paid close attention. The repetition was helping me match sounds to the orchestra sections. My brain is learning how to interpret the sounds—I have to "trust the process." And I have to walk before I can run!

JULY 5, POSTER DIARY

Many new cochlear moments on this day! This

morning I heard the receptionist talking to me from BEHIND the frosted glass window. When it happened, I answered her and said "Oh my gosh!" She opened the glass window, asking if I was all right. Of course I was all right, and I told her why—because I can hear now.

Later on, Ray and I played a video game with Randy. It was completely out of the ordinary that he would ask us to play the video game with him, so I was hoping it would be a positive experience for us all. Before the implant, this kind of activity would have been a one-sided affair—I could only offer one part of me at a time: play the game or converse with him. But today I did both.

It was so sweet having him explain to me how to play and being willing to share his gaming secrets with me so I could play smarter. Reciprocal interaction is something I have been missing for years! I savored every minute and every word we shared together. This afternoon I easily listened to talk radio for the first time in decades! Not only did I listen, I heard 100% of every overblown dramatic half-truth sentence spoken on the air for two straight hours.

The male and female voices were crispy and complete, stringing words along together like a rhapsody. The voices were host to all kinds of inflection, from comedies to tragedies, mimicking poetry, melody, and prose. It was hypnotizing! I was instantly attracted to talk radio like magnet to steel. Even on a radio, with no visual cues at all, the human voice is titillating and attractive, whether male or female. It's a connection between minds, apart from bodies. For me, talk radio was like getting to know another individual from the inside out through the power of words.

I could have become addicted overnight if I had taken any of it seriously! Lastly, I watched a movie tonight without focusing all of my attention on the captions. I can't recall the last time I watched a movie without reading words on the little lines at the bottom of the screen. I hope to break away from the things I depended on for so long—because I am no longer dependent on everyone around me!

JULY 6, POSTER DIARY

Today my cochlear "moment" grew into a cochlear marathon when I met up with Rosie at a large bookstore/coffee shop. This was another setting I had previously avoided, unless I planned to sit alone with a cup of joe. I have a large number of friends who frequent this particular place. A morning with the Coffee Shop Club (as I refer to them) was never my idea of a pleasant time—too many voices, too much background noise, too much blah, blah, blah!

Memories of being shut out of many delightful moments saddened me—but not for long because now I am in the Coffee Shop Club! We sat and talked for two hours while the other Coffee Shop Club members chatted away and the bookstore patrons hustled and bustled around us.

Then Rosie and I walked down the sidewalk to a little wine restaurant and shared a bottle of wine. We sat outside near the sidewalk, with a view of shoppers passing by and the Square. All the sounds worked together to create such sweet ambiance—the clicking of shoes on the pavement, the chatter of children on the center green, the voices of the other diners, the sound of the wine flowing from the bottle into the glass, and the tap of the knife cutting through cheese as it gently touched the plate. I felt like I was in a movie because the whole experience sounded so orchestrated and surreal!

Another two hours flew by as we enjoyed loads of laughs, interesting conversation, and wine. This day was such a gift! Silently, I thanked God once again for the gift of an ear that hears all of the things I have wanted to experience all my life. This is the best day of my life!

JULY 7, POSTER DIARY and SOCIAL NETWORK

Today I had lunch with another friend. I love eating out! It was a very big restaurant this time, but I did well after changing the setting on my remote assistant. We sat and talked for three hours. I can't think of a time when I was able to listen for **three** hours in all of my life. It was simply too exhausting. But today there seemed to be little or no effort involved—my focus was on the conversation, not figuring out each word. Being able to hear removes tension from the equation, making conversations totally enjoyable.

Then I had another appointment and decided to sit in the **back** of the waiting room. I opened a magazine, purposefully and confidently burying my head in the pages. As I was reading, someone called out my name and interrupted my thoughts. Looking up, I saw that the nurse was ready for me. I had heard her calling my name even though I was sitting in the back of the waiting room and not carefully observing my surroundings. The appointment was routine and I and did just fine on my own, without my husband translating or my sons helping.

JULY 8, POSTER DIARY

Every day is like an episode of "Those Amazing Sounds," which could be an imaginary series about learning how to hear after a lifetime of near deafness. Today's episode featured geese on the lake—and they were honking! But this cochlear moment did not end there. Ray and I had taken another moonlit walk, were holding hands, talking—and listening to the geese. Experiencing new sounds is wonderfully fresh and simple.

It's never too late to have another "first time." When we found our way back home, we invited Randy to play a board game with us and he obliged. Slowly we are creeping our way back into each other's hearts through direct communication such as the sharing of a game. Good times. This is the best day of my life!

JULY 9, BLOG

We made plans to meet up with our friends Rhonda and Ralph for dinner. This was my second time having dinner with another couple in a restaurant, but this time it was a Saturday night. And that meant huge crowds. Again I was nervous, a very bad habit I needed to break.

When we arrived at the restaurant, I was

shocked by the size of the place. The room was massive! As I noticed the crowd waiting for a table, I wondered what I had gotten myself into. It was nothing like anything I had ever done. I don't remember signing up for this, I thought.

Ray dropped me off so I could check in as he parked the truck. After checking in under Ray's name and realizing they did not offer vibrating pagers, I became very concerned that I would not hear the hostess call our name. I could feel a panic attack coming on—way deep down inside my gut. Ray was still parking our truck so this was up to me. This is what I had been wanting for so long—freedom and independence. Would I be able to handle it?

Ten minutes into the wait, Ray finally showed up. He, too, was surprised at the size of the restaurant as well as the crowded lobby. We moved as far away from the crowd as we could to talk about this evening's game plan. If it was too noisy for me to enjoy myself, we would change tables or just go somewhere else before ordering. We would talk it over with our friends to let them know the plans when they arrived. A few minutes later, as we waited for a table, I heard something in the distance—"Raymond, party of four. Raymond."

That was us—so I waved my hand in the air to let the hostess know we were on our way to her station. I turned to Ray, letting him know our table was ready. His response was "how do you know?"

"Because our name has been called." I told him.

"YOU heard that?" he exclaimed. The shocked look on his face only meant one thing. I can hear. Tonight, all night long, I heard everything just fine. I heard my husband, my friends, the waiter, even the man in the booth behind me ordering pinot grigio. This dinner was a night to remember—but my cochlear moment did not end there!

After dinner, we went back to Ralph and Rhonda's home, where we sat in the backyard chatting under the stars, illuminated only by the shimmer of a full moon. That moon. My moon. And yet, with all of our faces hidden in the darkness, we conversed. We talked family, we talked philosophy, and we talked friendship. This was another first! It was the only memory of its kind in my entire forty-six-year piggybank of memories. A simple celebration had turned out to be very grand. And it all happened under the moon who, for so long, saw me crying out for help.

And that is why this was the best birthday of my life.

JULY 11, POSTER DIARY

This morning I attended a workshop and learned about a new way to teach math, even though I don't teach math! The important thing is that I learned. There were six teachers in attendance and we interacted together perfectly, visiting, discussing, and learning. Feeling fine as I made my way home, I went out on a limb and listened to the voicemail. My bionic ear wirelessly and automatically linked into the phone line, making the voice messages go straight to my brain.

JULY 12, POSTER DIARY

More and more sounds are beginning to drive me crazy— what a wonderful feeling! Tonight, a loud clanking noise from the dryer brought out the detective in me. Each time I set the dryer going and walked away, the noisy clanking started up. I tried to ignore it but the sound reverberated through the kitchen, living room, and even traveled into the bedroom. It sounded as if there were a large metal spatula bouncing around in there, slamming against the metal barrel inside the dryer. But when I went back to check the dryer, there was nothing. I began pulling out each item one at a time. Again, nothing. I switched the dryer back on and at the very first clank, I yanked the door open to investigate.

Checking each article of clothing nearest to the barrel, there was only one item that could have been the cause of the clank. If I was right, when that item was removed and the dryer was switched on, it would spin in silence and I would have my answer. This was my newest cochlear moment.

After switching the dryer back on, it hummed quietly. I now had my answer. The clanking noise that had blasted through three rooms was nothing but a quarter. It was not as loud as I thought, but the mere sound of it was new—just like the first few days of hearing were so loud they were almost painful, so was this new clanking sound. Note to self: check pockets before doing the wash!

JULY 13, POSTER DIARY

Listened in on a speaker phone telephone conversation with granddaughter Taia. She isn't talking too much yet, but just a few words is all it took to rejoice in her angelic voice! As if she knew all I could intake were a few sentences, she delivered them and, just like that it was over. Short and sweet but I will never forget it. I can hardly wait to hear her voice in person.

Had a really nice conversation with the cashier at the grocery store. People can be quite pleasant when given the chance! I have been missing out on some of the nicest people in the world, the cashiers, the waitresses, librarians, clerks, secretaries, and even the mailman. It feels so good to be a part of the world I live in.

JULY 14, POSTER DIARY

I have been wondering if this day would ever happen! As I left an electronics store, the security alarm went off—it was a very unique and noticeable sound. Although

I had never heard it before tonight, I knew what it was right away. I stopped and slowly turned around. I was smiling at the young man walking toward me. He explained what happened—a tag had been left on my merchandise—and how he would correct the situation. Then we walked back in to the store together.

It had finally happened! I had been stopped at the security gate—I was so happy and so proud. My dignity would soon be restored. Calmly, I waited for the young man to take care of the situation. This time it was not my mistake walking away from the alarm—it was their mistake leaving the tag on. Courteously yet confidently, I said to the young man, "You really should do something about tags being left on merchandise." It was the best day of my life.

JULY 15, POSTER DIARY

MORNING

Feeling nervous and stressed because of a weekend family camping trip coming up—today. Old habits die hard, I suppose. Keeping things in perspective, I am anchoring on the trust and mutual respect between myself and my son, my three grown stepkids, my son-in-law, my daughter-in-law, and, of course, my lovely little granddaughters. I have never known them to be impatient with me. This is a mammoth weekend with many big steps to take.

AFTERNOON

Had lunch at a NOISY restaurant with most of the family—a group of eight adults, one adolescent, and one little girl. This was a new experience, the kind I had avoided for years, maybe even decades. Today, though, I was in their world—listening, chatting, and laughing with those around me. What I learned is that this kind of situation—where there are many people situated at one long table—is a setting where NOBODY can hear 100% of the conversations. I will never be able to do that. And guess what? Nobody else will either.

JULY 16, POSTER DIARY

We all went swimming today with the grandkids. I wore my processor into the water, knowing I did not intend to swim laps. As I walked down the steps of the pool, it was the beginning of another cochlear moment. I heard the water splashing, the children giggling, and the adults visiting with each other and with the kids. I cannot believe I am in their world! MY WORLD. I stood there in the water watching the action, breathing in the moment and hoping to capture it forever. I loved feeling so connected! It was the best day of my life!

JULY 17, POSTER DIARY

This morning when I woke up, the house seemed extremely peaceful. I took a few extra minutes lying in bed with the covers pulled up to my neck. I looked out the window, noticing the trees gently swaying and a squirrel running along the top of the fence. Turning over for a different view, I noticed the bathroom lights on and shadows moving in the light. These were all things I had seen hundreds of times. But something was different.

When my husband came out of the bathroom, he walked over to his dresser and opened the drawer, pulled out a pair of socks, and then pushed the drawer back into place. This was my ah-ha moment! Something had been missing from the scenario and now I knew what it was: sound. Something similar had just happened to me just a few weeks ago as I awoke to the bizarre sound of silence. But it had not been as intense as it was this morning!

Could it mean that I am fully acclimated to my new world? Probably not. I have been told my bionic journey will be lifelong, so realistically I have not adjusted to my whole new world, but I'm certainly accustomed enough to appreciate the sound of sounds! Before I switch the processor on in the morning, I am in my old world. But it's not such a bad thing any more, since I can leave that world when I want to. Ironically, my cochlear implant has taught me to appreciate the sound of silence.

JULY 18, POSTER DIARY

Today was iPod day! I worked with it for several hours, getting used to the sound of music. The attachment is interesting—one end goes into the iPod while the other end is hooked up to the processor behind my ear.

Then, voila, I'm jazzed! The music goes straight into my head, bypassing my ear. Sadly, my other ear is left out because the cord does not accommodate a hearing aid or a real ear—only a bionic one. So I use one ear bud. Who makes ear buds for one ear? I chuckled at my own bizarre uniqueness.

JULY 19, POSTER DIARY

Coffee with Elsie and Rosie, something I look forward to more than almost anything. The connection of friendship is what I have been missing for so long. Hearing their words and responding with my own, over and over and over is like a song with many different verses. Our conversations are a wonderful song of love!

★　　★　　★

The End Is the Beginning

This journey was a staggering exit from my world into yours, one that I survived by the skin of my teeth. It took forty-six years to find my way out. The rest of my life will be spent adventurously finding the way completely into yours.

Cochlear moments and surprising new sounds did not suddenly cease after just two months' time, but that is where this book ends. The journey itself continues and will continue each day I wake up in the morning with a burning desire to switch my life on. By doing so, I am making a choice to stay connected to this world, the world I now call home. My connection to life is truly an amazing grace, making every single day the best day of my life.

POSTSCRIPT

2017

In 2008 I discovered a way to connect with friends and family: Facebook. I had been using the Internet to connect with the world for a decade, but Facebook was different. It is a social network with a more personal, direct, and satisfying link between users. I eagerly anticipated posting, commenting, and instant messaging each day as I was starving for dialogue with those I cared about. Facebook was almost as good as a real conversation—and for me, it was as good as it was going to get. I was deeply grateful for the Internet, which led me to Facebook, and later to Instagram and LinkedIn. I hope to begin Twitter soon.

When I shared my cochlear implant activation on Facebook, the reaction was positive. Everyone sought to share in my experience. So I continued sharing every day—the thrill, bliss, and uniqueness of each new sound. In time the chunks of sound matured into speech that I could understand, and my verbal interchanges improved greatly. But people weren't saying what I had been hoping, or even expecting, to hear.

Much of what I had been struggling to comprehend was rooted in negativity, sarcasm and criticism of one person by another. People were belittling and ridiculing one another in virtually every setting.

In line at the grocery store I heard impatient customers behind me complaining about the cashier. At a restaurant I heard a waitress sarcastically addressing a diner, and then I heard the diners scoffing at the waitress! At a school I heard teachers belittling other teachers. On the walking trail I heard two women gossiping about someone's clothing being too tight. It saddened me to see such a dark side of the world I had always wanted to be included in. The power of negative speech was poison in the hearing world, which was now my world as well.

I struggled to focus on love, but I couldn't turn off the negativity that seemingly pervaded everything. Not adept at filtering out the impatience and unkindness, I absorbed it like a plant soaks in acid rain. Over the course of several months, without even knowing it, I was beginning to fit into the negative world. I had changed. Quietly I had become proficient at discourtesy and cynicism. Even Facebook, the magical place connecting me to my cherished social circles, was filling up with judgment and ridicule. The Internet was part of the poison! Social networks gave a voice to hatred that could instantly travel through the world. Facebook was turning to Hatebook.

I should have shut down my account when I saw what was happening, but I didn't. Instead I cursed my dog for barking one night. That's when I saw what was happening to me—I was angry that I could hear. I took a walk in the moonlight to reflect. Under a waning moon I decided it was time to purge my life of the poison that had been quietly seeping in.

Not just for myself, but for my kids and grandkids. How could I leave them a world where people tear each other apart? By doing nothing to stop this maliciousness, I was doing everything to encourage it. I thought about what I could do. I feel like an average human being, and while I'm definitely not a rocket scientist, I do know how to be kind, I know how to care, and I know how to love. That seemed like a good place to start.

Late into the night, I created a Facebook page designed to inspire positivity on the Internet. I called it *Building a Culture of Kindness.* Whether I would attract one user or many, I visualized a peaceful crusade instilling kindness among Facebook users to protect humanity from negative destruction. The crux of the plan was using kindness to fight the poison of the internet. We started with eight members. It's no coincidence that there were exactly eight people in my extended family who joined the movement. Three years later, with more than 5,000 followers worldwide, *Building a Culture of Kindness* is proof that care and compassion are important to many, not just a few. To this day I continue spreading the kindness movement that was initiated by my distressing reintroduction to the world of sound. Once praying to hear, I now pray to be heard as I am compelled to share the principles of hope and kindness.

This story is my connection to you, as my disability interleaves through each page like a needle pulling thread, pulling you into my world and me into yours —stitching our lives together. As it turns out, my life is made from fabric similar to yours. We wear different styles, but similar fabrics. We live different lives but face similar challenges. We sing different chords, but they harmonize beautifully into a song of kindness.

Amazing grace, how sweet the sound!

ABOUT THE AUTHOR

Susan Langlois began a new career in writing after retiring from public education in 2015. She also photographs the moon for stunning picture books and writes inspirational stories based on three decades worth of experiences with children. Susan's accomplishments include:

- Thirty years in education
- Reading Specialist, English as a Second Language (ESL) Specialist, Dyslexia teacher,and classroom teacher
- Master Teacher Mentor
- Five time Spring ISD Grant Winner
- Outstanding Houston Citizen by the North Houston Chamber of Commerce
- HEB Excellence in Education Lifetime Achievement Award Finalist
- Founder of "Once Upon a Time" Storybooks for Kids charity in Houston, Texas
- Heritage Elementary Teacher of the Year, Spring ISD
- Points of Pride Recipient
- Creator of *Building a Culture of Kindness*, a movement to spread kindness on Facebook.

FACEBOOK: Susan Langlois (author), Out of My World Into Theirs, Building A Culture of Kindness

BLUE MOON (LEFT), Susan Langlois

48535685R00130

Made in the USA
San Bernardino, CA
28 April 2017